# Galway on the Bay

Paintings by Derek Biddulph
Text by Dick Byrne and Peadar O'Dowd

Cottage
Publications

First published by Cottage Publications,
an imprint of Laurel Cottage Ltd.
Donaghadee, N. Ireland 2002.
Copyrights Reserved.
© Illustrations by Derek Biddulph 2002.
© Text by Peadar O'Dowd and Dick Byrne 2002.
All rights reserved.
No part of this book may be reproduced or stored
on any media without the express written
permission of the publishers.
Design & origination in Northern Ireland.
Printed & bound in Singapore.

ISBN 1 900935 25 2

## Dick Byrne

A native Galwegian, architect Dick Byrne was born in 1935 and was educated by the Presentation Nuns, the Patrician Brothers, the Jesuits and, latterly, U.C.G.

For many years he was closely associated with Taibhdhearc na Gaillimhe, the National Gaelic Theatre and during his time there he wrote twenty plays, pantomimes and pageants, all of which were performed on stage. In 1984 his play '*Auld Decency*' was performed by the Abbey Theatre Company in Dublin, while his pageant/play '*Where Once Stood Tribesmen*' was the feature play of the Quincentennial Celebrations in Galway that same year. In 1995 his play '*Dance of the Dinosaurs*' was a featured play in the Galway Arts Festival when performed by the Punchbag Theatre Company. In 1998 his first novel *Home for the Races* was published.

## Derek Biddulph

A resident of Galway for over forty years, Derek Biddulph became a painter almost by accident. It was to become so important in his life that eventually he gave up his job to devote himself completely to it.

Though he had little formal art training, Derek is widely recognised as one of the area's most accomplished artists. He has painted Galway in all its moods and in all its colours for many years now and is still discovering fresh angles from which to portray its ancient remains as well as its more modern face. Many of his paintings, either in oil or watercolour, are celebrations of the city's main features. Indeed it is fair to say that for a number of years Derek has been recognised as the premier visual chronicler of Galway, a city he has come to know and love intimately.

## Peadar O'Dowd

Local historian and newspaper columnist, Peadar O'Dowd, was born in Galway City and lectures in Office Information Systems in the Galway-Mayo Institute of Technology. He has also taught archaeology in Heritage Studies there, and is in much demand on the lecture tour and has spoken on such topics as '*The Great Famine*' in New York State, and on '*The Claddagh*' to the Royal Society of Antiquaries of Ireland in Dublin.

His published works include: *Down by the Claddagh, Galway Heart of the West, Old and New Galway, Vanishing Galway* and *Galway City* as well as many articles on local history and archaeology.

A highlight in a long career of heritage activities came when he, and his wife, Mary, were selected to represent Ireland at the Chicago Millennium celebrations.

# Contents

# Beginnings

God is good they say, and when he shaped this island of Ireland, he was at his most benign. Happy with its outline, he proceeded to stock the green isle with people on whom he bestowed a rather special gift. 'Imagination', they call it, and when it comes to the Irish today, they delight in its mental freedom, which adds greatly to their other virtue, 'the gift of the gab'!

Some call it blarney, but the Irish do find a story in the most mundane of things. Take, for instance, the aforementioned shape of Ireland itself. To anyone else, it looks like a rather small and dented rectangle on the very edge of Europe. Yet, ask that artful dodger in the corner of any Irish bar – you know, the one with the cap on the Kildare side – he will tell you otherwise. While mourning his vanishing porter, he will wipe the white satin from eager lips, which, of course, host a thousand tales. Well honed in the oral tradition, he will then tell you that the shape of Ireland represents a holy monk in the sitting position. Rugged Kerry coastlines are the feet of this mythical figure, while to the north, the hooded head is none other than the province of Ulster itself. To the west, the outward trust of Connacht are the arms of the holy man, folded tightly around his heart, centred rather appropriately in the vast county we call Galway.

County Galway, second only to Cork in size and the largest county in the province of Connacht, is an amazing tableau of changing land and seascapes. It is no stranger to the sea as the Atlantic sends a myriad of inlets to indent and beautify its long coastline, while the Gulf Stream comes to warm the heart of the county itself, Galway Bay. Renowned in song and story (Bing Crosby made his rendering of '*Galway Bay*' the top hit of 1950) this rectangular shaped bay, roughly ten miles by six miles in extent, is the most recognisable feature on Ireland's western shoreline. Sheltered at its entrance by the Aran Islands, this vast sheet of water has offered safe anchorage in its time to wind-swept Spanish galleons right down to the modern cruise liner of today. No other island decorates its centre, but smaller ones such as Mutton and Hare Islands guard the entrance to the estuary of the River Corrib on its northern shoreline, while the much larger isles of Tawin and Eddy fracture the symmetry of the eastern section of this giant bay.

While the shoals of herring, cod and ling, which figured so much in the catches of the former Claddagh fishing village on the River Corrib estuary, have long since vanished with the advent of outside trawling fleets in the 19th century, Galway Bay still holds large stocks of ray and dog fish. In season, mackerel are caught in their thousands from Galway City piers as well as from Ireland's longest promenade at Salthill, the city's seaside resort.

Meanwhile, above this important urban area, lies Lough Corrib, some 44,000 acres of clean freshwater, stretching nearly thirty miles from the city, the largest wild Brown Trout fishery in Europe today. Judicial as well as medical practices have been known to suffer in places as far away as Sydney and Montreal early every summer, as fans come there to dap Corrib May Fly above speckled beauties ordained to take the breath away. Filled with salmon, also, the lake's run of grilse in early summer is now a major European attraction. What other city hosts

such an amazing sight while these silver treasures rest beneath the appropriately named Salmon Weir Bridge as they make their way to spawning grounds many miles away? While heavy traffic shakes the piers of this ancient bridge, hundreds of these beautiful fish can be seen lying beneath in the crystal waters on the bed of a river, which has hosted countless generations of their ancestors since Irish time began. Lough Corrib beckons yet again – the call of nature is irresistible and it is here for everyone to see.

Just a four-mile journey up the short but powerful River Corrib brings these regal fish to the lake which, in reality, looks like an inland sea. In all, three major sections of this water, which stretches nearly thirty miles to the village of Cong on its northern shoreline, delight both fish and angler. Deeply bowered islands (365 if you are to believe the water's many legends), shallows, deeps, bays, inlets and peninsulas make this mighty water a visual pleasure for those who go down to lakes in boats.

The lower section, fed by the Clare River to the east, is mostly a shallow basin, its trout mainly confined to the rocky, stoney section to the west, while creatures of the mud and weed in summer in the eastern region offers more than the usual growth to pike of truly enormous proportions.

The next section of this remarkable lake is long and narrow, filled with small islands, bays, shoals and reefs, ideal topography for those who like to cast the fly for some of the richly speckled trout designed in heaven itself.

Then you come to it. The upper section of Corrib stretches out in front with huge deeps (down to 140 ft in places) and large islands and trout to go with them. Fly fishing is again the norm, but if you want that double-figure fish, troll your bait (a large roach will do) behind the boat here, but only pray your luck is in and the net is large enough! From the west, the inflowing Owenriff River acts as a marvellous natural nursery to both trout and salmon. There's more, of course, for up at Cong, thousands of eels swim their secret way north into Lough Mask through myriads of underground rivers, which flow unseen underneath the narrow limestone ithmus that separates these two great western lakes.

However, while Lough Corrib attracts more anglers than any other fishery in the country and visitors, as well as locals, ply its waters in pleasure and commercial craft alike, the geographer and landscape enthusiast will see this great lake in quite a different light. Some 12,000 years or so ago, when glaciers finally retreated from Ireland, a strange phenomenon took place. Rain fell for the first time on the emerging tundras and forests of this new land, and gradually filled the deep rifts left behind by abrasive ice. Thus, some 4,000 years later, Lough Corrib, the widest basin, was filled with freshwater and created a natural barrier between landscapes made different by vast geological changes undertaken millions of years before.

To the east of this vast waterway, in the immediate areas of mostly grass lands bounded by the urban centres of Headford, Tuam and Claregalway, the covering tropical seas of the Lower Carboniferous of 300 million years ago laid down vast tracts of calcium carbonate sediments, which later solidified into limestone. Today rich farm lands, filled mostly with cattle and sheep, overlie this limestone area, as exemplified by the vast field systems around the nearby town of Athenry, now made famous by Ireland's most rousing refrain, '*The Fields of Athenry*', sung by Irish sporting fans the world over.

Yet, dip your toes in western Corrib waters and the

vastly different landscape of Connemara greets the eye. Connemara, named after the Tribe of Conmaicne, who came to live by the mara, or sea, in prehistoric times, is one of Europe's last great natural wildernesses. Westwards from the picturesque Corrib angling village of Oughterard, great mountain ranges, countless small lakes and changing light patterns vie for attention. In the past, they have driven mere mortal artists such as Charles Lamb, Harry Kernoff and Maurice MacGonigal to sheer distraction. Yet it was William Makepeace Thackeray, who stayed a few memorable nights in Galway City in 1842, who first drew attention to the haunting beauty of these massive uplands when he noted in his work, *The Irish Sketch Book* :

*All one can do is to lay down the pen and ruminate, and cry beautiful! once more; and to the reader say, Come and see!*

Thus, when they come, using Galway City as a most convenient gateway, the first sight of the Maamturks stirs imagination in the native and visitor alike. Towering over 2,000 feet in height, these vast mountain monuments to creation, record even older geologic upheavals and metamorphic processes, reaching back in time to over 500 million years ago.

Out to sea, other geological marvels appear. Take for instance, the three Aran Islands; their geology as different to that of nearby Connemara as chalk is to cheese. Reaching only 300 feet at the highest points, these masses of pure limestone straddling the entrance to Galway Bay are, in reality, an extension of the Burren in County Clare. Representing Ireland's version of an empty moonscape, this huge Burren limestone plateau of the Carboniferous Period in County Clare on the southern shore of Galway Bay, led John Betjeman to write:

*Stony seaboard fair and foreign,*
*Stony hills poured over space,*
*Stony outcrop of the Burren*
*Stones in every fertile place ...*

Millions of years ago, the Burren stretched right across the entrance to the bay, forming what early records call Loch Lurgan, one of the three major lakes in ancient Ireland. Subsequently, the Atlantic burst through this massive limestone barrier, creating Galway Bay out of the lake and leaving the three highest points of the barrier as the Aran Islands. Evidence of this catalytic event is easily obtained along the shoreline west of Spiddal Pier, a dozen or so miles west of Galway City. A simple scattering of the sea sand with one's foot will reveal the stumps of ancient trees and even the soggy mess of bogs long since covered by the encroaching sea.

Nearby, all along the shoreline to Galway City, erratics, huge granite boulders deposited by glaciers on these open shorelines, tell other tales of course, for the main events of Irish geological time are easily ascertained in these ancient lands and shorelines of a place, which delights in the simple Gaelic term *Cois Fharraige* (Beside the Sea).

In the past, of course, these natural wonders could not be scientifically explained by experts of the day. The latter, however, were never lost for words. Imagination filled the gap of true knowledge, and myths and legends found sustenance in the minds of those eager to listen. Thus, tales of angry giants and Fir Bolg princes fill Galway lore for nearly every place. Take Greatman's Bay, jutting northwards from the shoreline beyond Galway Bay, between Carraroe and Gorumna Island. Here, according to Roderic O'Flaherty in his famous 17th century work, *West or H-Iar Connaught*, this Great Man was a giant who plundered all the vessels that sailed into Galway Bay. Not content with that, we are told, he even fished for whales!

*His angle-rod made of a sturdy oak,*
*His line a cable which in storms ne'er broke;*
*His hook he baited with a dragon's tail,*
*And sat upon a rock, and bobb'd for whale.*

Thankfully, such mythical beings often lend us their names, and what is more important, they now adorn some adjacent Galway City landscapes. Let us cast our eyes again on Lough Corrib and wonder, surely, at its name. Happily, the gods are at work here also, for the old name for this water, according to Sir William Wilde, (who with his son, Oscar, liked to dally in their western home in Moytura House at the northern end of the lake), was Loch Oirbsin, derived from the name of the sea-god, Oirbsi Mac Allid. The tale becomes more interesting, however, when we discover that Oirbsi was more commonly known as Manannn Mac Lir (The Son of the Sea), who also gave his name to the Isle of Man.

However, Galway has a larger claim on Manannn/Oirbsi, because, according to legend, his bones remain, perhaps just as long as his name, in these Corrib lands, because he was slain in battle by Uillin, grandson of Nuada of the Silver Hand, High King, no less, of the mysterious Tuatha De Danann. The hand-to-hand battle, according to legend, took place on the western shoreline of Lough Corrib, and if you want to know the exact location, look closely at the name of the village a few miles north of Galway City on the Oughterard Road. Moycullen it is called, and if you stretch the Gaelic version, *Magh Cuillinn*, just a little, you get the Plain of Uilinn – so there you are!

Lough Corrib is also full of legend and every one of its 365 islands will tell you a different tale if you only listen. A favourite, of course, is the strange sounding Inismicatreer, (The Island of the Son of the Three) in which we are told that an O'Flaherty chieftain was tempted to land there by three sirens, whose methods of enticement would certainly have put paid to Jason in his quest for the golden fleece. And what about Inishanbo (The Isle of the Old Cow), that tells of yet another mythical beast, which rose from the deep blue waters of the lake to give its magic milk to a starving O'Flaherty princess and her child.

Eastwards, and even here in the land of rolling farm lands and solid farmers, one will also find the mark of legend printed deep in the rural psyche as well on the landscape as old as time itself. Try, for instance, a gentle climb of Knockmea, that lonely hill beside the town of Tuam, overlooking the Corrib and

find that while doing so, you are never quite alone! For this is the Hill of Meadhbh, Queen of the Irish Fairies, who, according to legend, has sent many a changeling into an Irish home.

Enough, however, of this travelling through a county, whose breadth is half of that of Ireland itself. To Galway City, we need retire and seek a restful stroll along its many delightful waterways. Even here, the lure of legend demands attention as we pass by the Claddagh – its thatched homes now replaced by rows of terraced houses, its geese by the whitest swans in Ireland. These are no ordinary swans however, for local lore swears they are reincarnations of long dead *bádóirí* or boatmen, who plied the rough waters of Galway Bay in their brown sailed Claddagh Hookers.

Most of the old boats are gone now, their trade long since killed by commercial venture based simply on profit. Some remain of course, for the beauty of sail will never die and the thrill of the race has replaced the silver haul of herring over timbers blackened by time itself. Gone, however, are the old fishing superstitions – the sight of a red-haired woman only turns heads now – not the entire fleet back to base as in days of yore.

Happily, the renowned Claddagh Ring is still here – the wedding emblem worn by V.I.P.s the world over. Legend (what would we do without it?) has it that the first of its kind, through divine intervention, was dropped in 1596 by an eagle into the lap of Margaret Joyce, in thanks for her perseverance in building bridges all over Connacht in the 16th century. Ironically, this simple band of gold makes the Claddagh, now just a small enclave of the city, more famous than Galway itself.

At this stage, we may even wonder about the name of Galway itself. Again, let legend lend a hand. Imagination must come into play here also, for in our mind's eye the day is bright and cheerful, as the young maiden takes to the cool waters in a river, shortly to bear her name. She is no ordinary girl however, for she is Galvia, daughter of the local Fir Bolg chieftain. Headstrong to the extreme, she swims out into the current of this short, but powerful river, which relieves Lough Corrib of its excess waters. Today, these same waters are in spate. A sudden cry, and she is gone. Later, as her body is retrieved down by the Claddagh, a distraught father ordered that the river which took her life would bear her name. In time, the name transferred to the Norman town built upon its banks, and, today, Galvia has mutated to the more familiar Galway.

Thus, the name of Ireland's most western city was born in the water deep of legend itself. Naturally, the man with the cap in the corner of the bar will simply say, "Its gospel!" Not surprisingly, imagination, legend and place mingle well in these misty lands about the Corrib. Allow them to mix, and you find the West is very much awake.

Founded, it is said, by St Colman Mac Duagh, (Son of Duagh, a local noble) this establishment dates from around 610. Although born in this area the saint first went to the Aran islands where he established the little monastery and church at Kilmurvy, where the stone church still bears his name Teampall Mac Duagh.

The local king, Guaire of Gort, persuaded Colman to establish this monastery and undoubtedly assisted the construction, giving financial aid and by giving the site to the saint.

Although there are many church buildings in the enclosure, the site is dominated by the round tower, which stands some 33.5 metres high and is 17 metres in circumference. In common with the more famous tower at Pisa in Italy, it leans about two feet off plumb. This is due to the lack of a good foundation and it was found that the stones which support it are as little as two feet below the surface.

Notwithstanding this, it has stood for well over one thousand years and George Petrie, that great antiquarian, suggested that it was in fact built around 620.

There is an opinion that these towers were simply bell towers, while others believe that they were stores and places of refuge during attack. The fact that the entrance door to the tower is some 8 metres from the ground would give credence to the latter theory, and also the round shape is notoriously difficult to damage with the simple siege tools of the age, which would have been timber battering rams. One way or another, the tower was certainly put to the test as the monastery was attacked twice by Vikings in 866 and again in the early 10th century and as often again by local marauders. The tower was restored in 1878/79 to its present condition. Also in the complex is the 10th century Cathedral or *Teampall Mór Mac Duach;* O Heyne's Church, built in the early part of the 13th century; the Small Church, probably of a similar date; the Church of John the Baptist, possibly from the 12th century; Our Lady's Church from the 12th century (although containing a cross slab of an earlier date); *Teampall Beg Mac Duach* now only visible as a foundation and the Bishop's or Abbots House, which is to be seen on the south of the car park.

# Kilmacduagh

This 15th/16th century tower house was built by the de Burgo family who held it until the end of the 17th century when it became part of the Perrse and Martyn family lands. Eventually it became part of the Gregory estate from which it was bought by W.B. Yeats, the great Irish poet, and restored as a residence in the early part of the 20th century.

Yeats discovered, and fell in love with the area when visiting Lady Gregory at the nearby Coole Park in the course of the establishment of the Celtic Literary Revival movement. It is recognised that Yeats wrote some of his best works here and fancied himself as somewhat of a Lord of the Manor.

The influence of Yeats and Lady Gregory, John Millington Synge, Seán O Casey, Bernard Shaw, Douglas Hyde, Edward Martyn, Oliver St John Gogarty, AE (George Russel) and the others of their movement was astonishing. At no other time in the history of the state has there been such a cultural revolution. This area and the people living in and around it were the inspiration for much of the work.

This influence on those early playwrights cannot be over-estimated. The language spoken in the plays of Yeats and Lady Gregory in the early days of the Abbey Theatre became known as 'The Kiltartan Dialect' or even Kiltartanese after the barony in which Thoor Ballylee is situated.

Yeats was not the only poet to be influenced by the place as, a century earlier, the famous Anthony Raftery, the blind Irish poet, fell in love with a local girl from Ballylee and composed one of his greatest love songs *Máire Ní Eidhin* in her honour.

Thoor Ballylee is now an interpretative centre for Yeats and his works and contains a tea room and tourist information centre. In the winter of 1999/2000 the entire ground floor was flooded when the river burst its banks.

# Thoor Ballylee

This impressive tower house was built in 1520 on the site of an earlier fort of the ancient Gaelic King Guaire who gave it his name. Originally in the hands of the Martyn family, one of the tribes of Galway, it was sacked by the followers of Cromwell and for many years fell into disrepair. Seeking to emulate Yeats at Thoor Ballylee, Oliver St John Gogarty purchased it from Edward Martyn, but never had the money to do anything with it. He sold it, and in the late 1950s it was purchased by the eccentric Lady Cristobel Ampthill, who was famous in British legal circles sometime in the 1930s as the second immaculate conception. She won succession rights for her son when her husband had claimed to have never consummated their marriage. She argued successfully that she became pregnant by taking a bath after him in the same bath water.

She began the long and difficult task of restoring the tower house, which took her the best part of ten years. She then sold it to its present owners, Shannon Development Co., who use it as a visitor centre, and arrange performances and medieval banquets there from May to October twice nightly at 5.30 p.m. and 8.45 p.m.

Kinvara is a beautiful and historic old fishing village with brightly painted shops and houses, famed for its restaurants and bars which crowd around the picturesque harbour filled with sailing and fishing craft of every size and age.

Every year between the 11th and 15th of August, the famous *Cruinniú na mBád* takes place. This is a regatta of traditional sailing craft known as hookers, some of them over one hundred years old. The event is as much a festival of music and fun as it is a regatta, and it has been said that so much porter is drunk here every year that the boats could float on it.

# Dunguaire Castle, Kinvara

Perhaps the most spectacular house site in the entire county is that enjoyed by the former seat of the St George family at Tyrone, near Kilcolgan.

This massive pile dates back to 1779, and it's now empty window sockets look out in every direction over miles of this part of County Galway. Designed, it is thought, by John Roberts of Waterford, for Christopher Ffrench St George, there can be no doubt that this was the house of a substantial landlord, and the St Georges were just that. In all they had over 25,000 acres of land in many parts of Galway, Roscommon and other counties.

Described as three storey over basement with seven bays and a breakfront, the building is constructed of almost perfect ashlar limestone blocks, some of which were robbed out in recent times.

The house is now a ruin, having been burned out by the local I.R.A. in common with many other fine houses, in a flurry of patriotism in 1920. The fact is that the only occupant of the house at the time was an old family retainer and by then the family had moved on in any case. In fact Christopher, who built the house in 1799 passed it to his son in 1801 and moved in to the nearby Kilcolgan Castle with his mistress, with whom he proceeded to have a large 'Bar Sinister' family. It is believed that this house and its family was the inspiration for the book '*The Big House at Inver*' by Edith Somerville of Somerville and Ross fame after a visit that her cousin and co-author Violet Martin had made there in 1912.

Many dreamers have pondered the possibility of restoring this house, but it would take very deep pockets indeed to achieve this.

# Tyrone House and Kilcolgan Castle

Ardfry House probably replaces an earlier 17th century house. Thomas (Black) Blake whose family owned the land since 1612 died on his tobacco plantation in America around 1711 and his wife Honora sold the plantation and returned to Ardfry with her son and daughter. The present house was built in the latter part of the 18th century for Joseph Blake. Prior to the Blake occupation, the de Burgo's had a castle nearby, some of the ruins of which are still to be seen. After the death of Joseph Blake in 1806, the house remained empty and deteriorated until, in 1826, it was refurbished and had its style changed by the addition of the gothic features and crenellation which remain to this day.

May, the second wife of Errol Augustus Blake, whom he married after his first wife died in 1889, had a bad gambling habit and it is said that she sold the lead off the roof to settle her gambling debts. After that it was all down hill for the house, with water running down through it and rotting the floors away. In the 1970s, for a short few weeks, it got a new lease of life when it was re-roofed for the film *The Mackintosh Man* that featured the actor Paul Newman. In the course of the film the house was set on fire and the roof burned off again.

For many years the last three of the Blake sisters, known affectionately as 'the little mice' lived in the steward's house in the grounds.

### Galway Bay Sailing Club

This club was revived from an earlier club in the late 1960s by a group of enthusiasts who sailed in little sailing craft every Wednesday evening and Sunday morning on Lough Atalia. In the mid 1970s they became more ambitious and moved to the present site which was part of the Rinville House estate. The present clubhouse was built around 1977 and the club has flourished since this time with more members now than ever. The many boats standing at moorings make a pleasant picture, much appreciated by visitors and artists alike.

# Ardfry House and Galway Bay Sailing Club

*As I went down to Galway town,*
*To seek for recreation,*
*On the 17th of August,*
*My mind being elevated,*
*There were multitudes assembled*
*With their tickets at the station,*
*Their eyes began to dazzle*
*And they going to see the races.*

Thus goes the opening verse of the old broadsheet ballad, which is probably contemporaneous with the races themselves, since the first ever race meeting at the Ballybrit Racecourse was held on the 17th of August 1869.

The Galway Plate was first run on this day over a distance of two and a half miles for a prize fund of one hundred gold sovereigns, an enormous amount of money in those days, and was won by Absentee, with W. Bell in the saddle. The first race was run by the gentry many of them members of the famous Galway Blazers Hunt, which is still in existence and going strong in Craughwell in the county.

The first committee was chaired by Lord William St Lawrence, and counted amongst its members the Marquess of Clanricarde, Sir Valentine Blake, George Morris of Spiddal, an ancestor of Lord Killanin who himself was a member of the race committee until his recent death.

Later the date of the races changed to the first week of August, and the Galway Plate was run on Wednesday and the Galway hurdle was run on the Thursday, and on Friday the whole show moved down to Tuam for what was generally regarded as the third day of the races.

When the Tuam Racecourse closed down, the Friday meeting was transferred to Galway and the meeting became a three-day event. Nowadays it is a full week long and there are two other meetings one in September and the other in October.

The Galway Race week is now one of the biggest festivals of any sort in the country and is responsible for injecting millions of euro into the City's tills.

# Galway Races

The word Menlough, meaning little lake in Irish, give the area and the castle their name. The building dates probably from Elizabethan times, and it is possible that the northern wall and the communicating parts of the eastern and western walls, which are substantially thicker than the rest, form part of the original tower house which belonged to Sir Thomas Coleman between 1574 and 1598.

By 1600 the house had passed to Valentine Blake who became Mayor of Galway in 1611 and again in 1630. In 1622 he was created a Baronet, and his descendants carried the title and indeed the name Valentine into the 19th century. The castellated addition to the house was built in the early 18th century and later that same century the most notorious of the Valentine Blakes, the 12th baronet, added more decorative features to the castle. This Sir Valentine was a notorious big spender and gambler who eventually spent most of his time evading his creditors who gathered at his gate and literally laid siege to the house. He discovered however that it was not allowed to serve summonses or writs on a Sunday so on this day he would sally forth to his club (The Galway County Club) then in Eyre Square and make merry with his friends. He also discovered that writs couldn't be served on a Member of Parliament nor while on water, and so he used the river when canvassing his constituents, and was known to talk to them while standing in his boat on the river. Another device he used while canvassing was to quickly cross the river in a boat and take a carriage on the other bank and proceed with his business on the other side of the river. These games inevitably earned him the title 'Sunday Boy' Blake. He was successful in his endeavours and became an M.P. for the area, from 1812 until 1820 and again from 1841 until 1847 when he died in Paris.

On July 26th 1910 the house suffered a disastrous fire in which the elderly Lady Ellen Blake and one of her servants died.

# Menlough Castle

This fine mock-Tudor building first opened its doors to its first batch of students in 1849. The building was begun in 1846 and continued during the worst ravages of the great famine, during which period the population of the whole island fell by over two million. One million died from hunger and another million flooded out of the country in desperate search for work and food.

Sir James Graham, introduced the bill to establish the Queens Colleges in May of 1845, but Galway was not a primary location chosen for one of the Colleges. It was agreed that Cork, in the South, would be a location for one and Belfast, in the North, another, but the choice between Limerick and Galway to serve the West of Ireland was not made. Sir Valentine Blake of Menlough Castle, the M.P. pressed the case of Galway, being that it was in his constituency. Eventually Sir Robert Peel, the Prime Minister, agreed with Galway as the venue and the die was cast.

When it started in 1849 the College had faculties in Arts, Medicine, Law and Engineering, and there were Professorships in Natural History, Chemistry, Celtic Studies, Modern Languages, English Law, Agriculture, Political Economy, Engineering Studies, Medicine and Surgery.

It is hard nowadays to imagine what an enormous undertaking it was to build such an establishment. Of course there were some inter-college jealousies, and a certain rumour gained some credence that the plans were 'mixed up' and that the brick college in Belfast was the one intended for Galway, and the fine limestone edifice we now see was intended for Belfast. Of course there is no foundation to such a tale, since brick never gained any architectural hold in Galway and Limestone was readily and cheaply available in almost every field. The university campus now covers most of the west bank of the river Corrib in many varied modern buildings and the original building primarily houses administration offices.

The student population of the College has grown from the initial 68 students of 1849 to in excess of 12,000 today.

# National University of Ireland, Galway

From the earliest of times, it was the Collegiate Church of St. Nicholas which provided the cathedral needs of the Catholic community of Galway City, but with the arrival of the Reformation it changed hands and has since been the Church of Ireland headquarters in Galway. The pro cathedral or the Parish Church of St. Nicholas was the next home of the diocese of Galway, but it was hopelessly cramped and far too small on ceremonial occasions. It had long been hoped to build a proper cathedral here, and the late Dr. Browne, who was consecrated bishop in 1937 made it his life's ambition to achieve this. Achieve it he did, for he lived to see his dream fulfilled and to see this great limestone edifice rising from within the foundations of the old Galway gaol, within the area of whose walls it now stands. Designed by the late John Robinson, an architect from Dublin, the building was completed and was consecrated by Cardinal Cushing of Boston on 15th of August 1965 as the 'Cathedral of Our Lady Assumed into Heaven and St. Nicholas', thus keeping the City's link with its patron saint.

As an architectural piece there is no doubt that it is a massive structure, but its appearance is perhaps a little too massive, with more emphasis on stone than light. It might be described generally to be of Romanesque style, but there are several anomalies. There can be no doubt however that it is a triumph of the mason's art, and the joinery of the barrel vaulted ceiling is first class.

As a cathedral it fulfils all that is required, and it provides a fitting tomb for its creator Dr Michael Browne who is buried within its walls.

An interesting collection of medieval carved panels exists on the wall of the Chapel of St. Nicholas (on the left inside the Salmon Weir Bridge entrance). These represent the Holy Trinity, and were removed from the 18th century pro cathedral, and had been removed before that from the Collegiate Church of St Nicholas in the early 17th century. This one might say is a tangible link between all three churches.

# Galway Cathedral

Galway has always been a market town, at least for some 600 years or more, and not one but several markets abounded in its streets. There was a market for sea fish and another market for freshwater fish, as well as a market for potatoes and one for cattle and horses. The present market, which takes place every Saturday, is situated in Lombard Street, Church Lane, and Market Street, formerly North Street. For many years the market was in somewhat of a decline with only vegetables, fowl and eggs for sale. Thankfully, nowadays, with the advent of many people from different cultures and countries, all of them seeking to return to the land and to sell their wares, the market has taken on a magnificent cosmopolitan air, with everything imaginable for sale, ranging from spices to several different types of olive and literally dozens of cheeses.

The market itself wraps around the railed-in enclosure of the Collegiate Church of St Nicholas which is the jewel in the crown of the Galway City medieval buildings. Begun in 1320, the church was elaborated upon and enlarged by the wealthy burghers of the town, in an effort to show how they loved their God and, perhaps, also to show the world at large just how wealthy they really were. Ongoing works have taken place on this fine building, and a major redevelopment took place in the 1950s and again in the 1980s, leaving it today to be one of the finest of all medieval churches in the country. Christian worship has taken place there continuously since 1320, the only exception being when Cromwell's forces defaced it and used it as stabling for their horses.

Originally a Catholic Church, with the Reformation it became a Protestant church and is now one of the finest Church of Ireland buildings in the country. It is dearly loved by all Galwegians of every denomination, all of whom regard it as Galway's church. Facing it across the Market Square is a small street known now as Bowling Green. It was here that Nora Barnacle, the wife and inspiration of James Joyce was born. Her family home is now preserved as a heritage centre and is worth a visit.

# Galway Market and St. Nicholas's Church

This mis-named structure is part of the fortifications built in 1584 to protect the harbour or docks, which were in those times situated on the north of the arch. According to the famous 1651 map of Galway there were evidently four arches, all of them resembling the present closed arch or the blind arch as it is known. These were more than likely used as dockside warehouses to hold cargoes of wool, tallow or salted fish for export, or barrels of wine awaiting transport to the city's many vast wine cellars. The long wall (Long Walk) was built to assist in the hauling of ships into the port against the flow of the quay stream. Sometime in the middle of the 18th century one of the arches, probably the second one, was opened up to assist access to the wall and eventually to give access to the new dock at the end of the walk. Arches 3 and 4 were probably demolished in the building of the large house which now houses the Galway City Museum, although the original wall with its heavy corbels still exists behind this house.

The Galway fish market existed in front of the arch right up until about the 1950s and it was common to see Claddagh women with their baskets and barrels of fish for sale on Wednesdays and especially on Fridays. Another feature was the row of salted Ling laid on the walls to dry in the sun.

The name 'Spanish Arch' comes from the romantic notion that Spanish sailors strutted their stuff in and around the arch during the early trading days between Galway and Spain, although it is more likely that the last concentration of Spanish sailors seen there were the unfortunate survivors of the Armada wreck in Galway bay in 1588 who were captured and executed by order of Queen Elizabeth I in Galway city. Their bodies are laid to rest in Fort Hill Cemetery.

# The Spanish Arch

One of the city's old market streets, Market Street Lower begins in the south with the fine early 18th century five bay, three storey over basement, limestone ashlar building known as Mayoralty House. Although it did house a number of mayors named Daly, it was not, as has often been assumed, the official residence of the mayors of Galway.

The street itself is described as being 'the little market' in the famous 1651 map of the city, and had in the middle of the street, at the junction with Flood Street, an altar erected by the Dominicans for the Corpus Christi procession, which was perhaps the major religious festival in the old city.

About half way along its length there is a junction with Middle Street, and a little further on a cross junction with High Street and Quay Street (formerly Watergate Street) at which is one of the most notable and interesting buildings in this part of the city, known nowadays as Seaghan Ó Neachtain's bar.

Although much altered over the years this house is a fine example of a 16th century house of a well-to-do owner. This was the town house of 'Humanity Dick' Martin M.P. of Ballynahinch, so known as he helped to pass the anti-cruelty to animals legislation through parliament. Also known as 'Hair trigger Dick' he was a renowned good shot on the duelling field.

In 1928, when assisting in the establishment of the Taibhdhearc, Michael Mc Liammóir and Hilton Edwards were in 'digs' in this house and shared the room with the fine oriel window, which juts out from the first floor to overlook all four directions. They complained that although the landlady treated them royally, and fed them well, she kept trying to foist her daughter off on one of them. Little did she know!

# Cross Street and Quay Street

Perhaps one of the best known bookshops in the world, with devoted customers as far apart as Iceland and China, Kenny's grew from a very humble beginning when Maureen and the late Des Kenny graduated from U.C.G. in 1940 and with every penny they could find, decided to open their bookshop in a battered old 15th century shop building in High Street.

Over the years the business has prospered and, although Maureen still keeps a watchful eye on the proceedings every day, the business is now in the capable hands of her sons and daughter. Indeed some of the third generation of the family are now employed in various corners of the empire.

In the late 1970's Kenny's purchased the Taibhsín, from Taibhdhearc na Gaillimhe in Middle Street to the rear of the main building, and this now houses the well-known Kenny Art Gallery, which is run by Tom Kenny, son of Maureen and Des, local wit, raconteur and Galway historian.

In recent times the entire building, much of it 15th century with 18th and 19th century additions, has been completely overhauled and now houses probably the most comprehensive collection of Irish books and paintings to be found under any one roof anywhere in the world.

More than just a bookshop and gallery, Kenny's has become a hangout for writers and artists from all over the world, where poets and writers wander and find themselves inspired by the paintings, and where painters find inspiration in some of the poems. This is evidenced by the hundreds of photographs of artists and writers to be found on every free bit of wall space in the building. This is where the muses live. They can be seen, smelt and even touched in four floors of art, literature and history.

# Kenny's Bookshop

**P**ronounced 'thigh v yark', this is the National Gaelic Theatre, and Galway's oldest established Theatre Company.

In 1928 a group of academics and Gaelic scholars sought to establish a Gaelic, or Irish language, theatre and wrote to the minister of finance for assistance in the project. Ernest Blythe (who was then the minister for finance and was later to become the director of the Abbey Theatre Company) told them that if they could find a good Irish play and somebody with Irish to direct it he would consider their request. A young actor called Michael Wilmore, who was travelling with the famous Anew McMaster theatre company, told them that he had such a play so they wrote and asked him to come and see them.

He replied using his new Irish name, Micheál McLiammóir and arrived with his new friend Hilton Edwards to show them the play *Diarmuid agus Gráinne* and they were both hired. Blythe was true to his word and McLiammóir's play was produced and performed in that same year in what was then the Augustinian (or Fr. Crotty) Hall. McLiammóir and Edwards went on to form their own theatre at the Gate in Dublin later that same year.

The company has continued to survive and prosper from that day to this, performing original Irish plays and translations from other languages. Memorable productions included Shaw's *St Joan*, which helped to establish the career of the leading lady Siobhán Mc Kenna. Bertholt Brecht's *Threepenny Opera*, Beckett's *Waiting For Godot'* O Gráda's *An Triail* and Mc Mahon's *Honey Spike* are some of the shows which spring to mind.

Many well known actors cut their theatrical teeth in the Taibhdhearc. As well as the aforementioned Siobhán, these include Walter Macken who was also a famous author and playwright and who started his literary career in this venerable institution. Sean McClory who went on to become a Hollywood actor, Mick Lally who has gained fame as Miley in the R.T.E. soap *Glenroe*, Peadar Lamb of the Abbey Theatre and many others.

The building was altered somewhat in the 1960s and renovated totally in 1978 and again in 1985 when an extra storey was added to produce its present configuration.

The theatre is also a facility for other visiting companies who may perform in any language.

# Taibhdhearc Na Gaillimhe

Described by some as the lungs of Galway, Eyre Square began its existence as the town green, known as Meyrik Square. In 1710 it was presented to the city for all time by Alderman Edward Eyre, who was Mayor of the city at that time.

On the 1651 map it is shown as a jousting green where folk came to play, and, more somberly, it shows the gallows, where people were hanged.

By the 18th century it had become the recreation space for the citizens of Galway where people came to picnic and relax with their families and friends. In early Victorian times it was enclosed by high wrought iron railings. Highlight of the year for many in the 20th century was the annual arrival of Toft's amusements around the races time, with Chairoplanes, swings, dodgems and all the fun of the fair.

The Browne Doorway, which now stands in apparently pointless isolation was moved here from the ruins of the Browne mansion in Lr. Abbeygate Street in 1905 to provide a suitable entrance to the park which, when there were railings, it did admirably.

It was here in 1963, a few months before his assassination in Dallas that John F. Kennedy gave one of his Irish speeches. A few years later, in some perverse rush of blood to their collective heads, the City fathers decided to 'modernise' it and, by removing the railings and cementing in the beautiful flower garden which was the pride of the city, reduced it to its present state.

The friendly little statue of Galway's most loved writer Pádraic Ó Conaire by Albert Power was erected in 1935 while the large fountain, which depicts the sails of Claddagh Hookers in the wind, was executed by Éamonn Ó Doherty and was erected to celebrate the city's Millennium in 1984. The cannon were presented to the city by the army following the Crimean War in 1856.

A word of warning, the city fathers are at it again, and it is proposed to demolish the present square and turn the entire area, or most of it, into a pedestrian plaza. Watch this space!

# Pádraic Ó Conaire Statue, Eyre Square

The Lynch family, one of the oldest and most powerful in Galway, came to Ireland with Hugh de Lacy in 1185 and, being strong and influential, were up front when the goods and lands of the Irish were being divided out. They gave the city its first mayor, Pierce, in 1484 and his brother Dominic was the second mayor. Down the centuries, until Cromwell finally decimated their power in the city, they gave the city more mayors, sheriffs and wardens than any other family.

The house, or castle, itself is a bit of a conundrum, since it is generally accepted to have been built in the late 15th or early 16th century, yet there is no sign of it on the Barnaby Gooch map of 1583 nor on the Speed map of 1610. It looms large, however, on the famous 1651 map so there is a possibility that it was smaller than it is now in its early days, not rising perhaps more than two or three storeys. As the family and the city prospered it may have been raised to its present four floors. The castle abounds in magnificent and elaborate carvings, which include the arms of Henry VII (1485-1509) and the arms of the Earl of Kildare, as well as those of the Lynch family itself. One of the carvings shows a monkey carrying a baby giving rise to the legend that a pet ape rescued a child from a blazing building, however this a familiar motif in early buildings and the tale appears without substance.

On the Abbeygate Street elevation are two gantry stones, which would have supported a beam and pulley block to raise provisions up from the street to the kitchen. There is also a disused garderobe (a toilet or refuse chute) down which various types of refuse would have been dumped unceremoniously on the passing populace. Some of the other buildings to the rear of the castle in Abbeygate Street may have been the courtyard and outbuildings, stables etc. for the castle.

The castle itself has been much altered over the centuries and now houses a branch of the Allied Irish Bank. It is probably in the best condition it has ever been at present, and the A.I.B. have mounted an exhibition in the foyer where there is also a very fine medieval fireplace.

# Lynch's Castle

As one might expect in a city as old as Galway, there are a great number of medieval remains of buildings to be found. The streetscape of the old part of the town has changed little in five hundred years or more, a fact that can be seen clearly on the early maps, particularly those of Speed from 1610 and also the famous 1651 map. Amongst the most common relics to be found are old stone chimney-pieces or fireplaces. Many of these are quite elaborate and contain as their keystone elaborately carved coats of arms, the so-called 'Marriage stones', although many of these stones were apparently removed and placed over front doors at a later date.

The particular stone in this painting is in its original location, and I can say this with some conviction since I first discovered it many years ago behind layers of wallpaper and plaster myself while doing a routine survey for the then owner of the property. However, the room that contains this large impressive fireplace (first floor of the Druid Lane restaurant in Quay Street) is tiny and proves beyond a doubt that the building and the others to the left of it were once the same building. This can be verified by examining the front elevation of the buildings in question, which start at the Wooden Heart toyshop. This is also visible on the 1651 map.

Most of these fireplaces were situated in the great hall of the buildings that contained them. Therefore if one imagines the entire first floor of the buildings mentioned one can get the impression of the size of this great hall. Many other fireplaces such as this were removed from the first floor and brought down to the ground floor where they could be seen, and perhaps used more practically. Those in the Kings Head pub for instance. There is a particularly fine example in the very top floor of Taafe's Bar in Shop Street which also contains the remains of a fine stone oven, and appears to be in situ, as this attic room once extended over the adjoining building which now houses Griffin's bakery. There are enough of these fine relics to be the subject of a study in their own right.

# Medieval Fireplace

Nowadays it is hard to imagine, when one visits the Quays, Galway's cathedral to the god Bacchus, that this massive and impressive structure is quite modern and only arrived in its present configuration in the late 1980s and early 1990s. The original pub was known as Delia Lydon's and is preserved virtually intact inside the front left-hand door. This was an old 19th century bar which had only two rooms and could accommodate, on a crowded night, about thirty persons. It was common enough to see a row of little old shawled women drinking glasses of stout in the back room or parlour, while 'Galway John' Ward, the last king of the itinerants would stand and look dreamily from him in the front bar, sipping a pint, when he had done his round of chimney sweeping in the city.

The right hand front door, which now leads into the main area of the bar, once The Pedlar Bookshop, specialising in second hand books, previously held Elwood's pawnshop. This most important enterprise, until the affluent seventies, was Bank and Credit Union to the poor people of the city. Suits and shawls would often be pawned on a Monday to provide food and sustenance for the week, until whatever wages would be paid on Friday, when they could be bought back again. Also very popular with university students in need of a few pints, many was the item deposited there, never to be recovered, by thirsty undergraduates.

A famous local dance band musician, fond of the ponies and the drink, would pawn his saxophone there most Mondays after the weekend's gigs and reclaim it on a sub when the next dance came along. He pawned it so often that Mrs Elwood didn't even bother to look at it, only to deposit it in its case on the shelf every Monday. One weekend when he hadn't reclaimed it for a couple of weeks, she became suspicious, and opening the case found it to be full of stones.

The Quays is a pretty spectacular establishment and houses not only a bar, but also a good restaurant, and on the first floor a most successful night club. Well worth a visit.

Quays Pub

Until very recently this lane or narrow street was in a ruinous state and was hardly a place where anybody would wish to walk. One was likely to encounter several stray cats and dogs, walking was extremely hazardous and the smell of decaying fish filled the air. Now, however, thanks to the recent prosperity of the city this old street has been very well restored, and now houses some of the city's trendiest bars, restaurants and cafés.

No doubt called after the Kirwan family, one of the fourteen famous tribes of Galway, this lane once housed a convent for the Presentation Nuns who opened a school there in 1808. Some time before this it also contained a theatre which was set up by 'Humanity' Dick Martin to indulge his wife's passion for acting. The famous Irish patriot Theobold Wolfe Tone appeared in a play there with Mrs Martin and it was rumoured that they may even have been an item.

Much of the original fabric of the houses can still be seen as it was carefully preserved in the restoration of these buildings in recent times, and in many cases modern copies were manufactured in stone to match those beyond repair.

The lower part of this lane, which extends from McDonagh's famous seafood restaurant on Quay Street to Goya's Café (where an almost sinful chocolate cake is served), was once known as Martin's Mill Lane and is so described in the index attached to the 1651 map.

The lane is much-beloved of painters and visitors with cameras, as it still has the original feel of a 16th-17th century street and it is a firm favourite on the tourist walking tours of the city.

# Kirwan's Lane

It seems hard to believe it now, but the Galway Arts Festival will be celebrating its Silver Jubilee this year (2002).

The brain child of Ollie Jennings, an enterprising and wheeler dealer student of U.C.G. at the time, who got together with artist Ted Turton and between them they hatched up what was the first 'real' arts festival in the country. True, there were theatre festivals and the like in Dublin and other places, but for 'All the stops out, no holds barred, lets have loads of Craic, music, dance and whatever you're having yourself' the Galway Arts festival took the people of Galway and introduced them to the delights of the world.

Artists come here year after year from China, France, Mexico, Spain, Australia etc and delight us, sometimes anger us, even frighten us but above all entertain us. One of the first big gigs was the travelling theatre company Footsbarn, who ,were followed by the colourful, scary Els Comediants and more theatre companies, painters, sculptors and actors than it is possible to name.

One of the most surprising developments of the festival was the founding of Macnas, Galway's own street Theatre Company, by Ollie Jennings, Páraic Breathnach, Tom Conroy and Peter Sammon. Macnas provides the centrepiece for the festival every year with a loud, colourful, brash, in-your-face parade through the centre of Galway with drums banging, bands playing, fire eaters blazing, floats of all shapes and sizes floating, flying, jumping and jiving. Through a deal with FÁS, the national apprenticeship board, Macnas now teach skills such as float building, theatre art, papier maché and all of the skills it takes to provide such entertainment. This has given rise to many Macnas clones in other towns all over the country and even abroad. Long may they continue.

# Galway Arts Festival

The Salmon Weir is at the heart of the city of Galway and has been, for perhaps a thousand years, one of the main natural assets of the City. It may be that the natural phenomenon of the returning wild salmon every year to this place was one of the principle reasons for the original establishment of a town on this site. It is something that has been jealously guarded for many years and the granting of the fishery rights goes back all the way to Henry III who granted the right to the earl of Ulster which then, through marriage, passed to the de Burgo's, from whom it was later stolen, or seized, by Richard II. Walter de Bermingham of Athenry acquired them towards the end of the fourteenth century. Eventually the de Burgo's got them back again but they were the subject of much haggling, claim and counter claim over the succeeding centuries. As well as a salmon fishery, of course, there has always been a highly successful eel fishery and the famous King's gap is visible on the earliest maps of the city.

A favourite pastime for generations of locals and tourists alike has been to lean over the parapet of the Salmon Weir Bridge to watch the incoming salmon rest in the waters below and sometimes to see an angler, waist deep in water, land one of these silver beauties.

In recent times the Fishery was the property of the Barbers of Billingsgate in England and one of that family actually lived with his family in the fishery house (now the Galway County Club) until the 1970s. The fishery is now in the possession of the Western Regional Fisheries Board and anybody can fish there if they have a licence and pay the daily fee.

The modern hydraulic weir is of recent construction and replaces an early mechanical one. This gives greater control over the flow of the river and can prevent flooding in times of severe rainstorm.

The Salmon Weir Bridge might have been known as Galway's own 'Bridge of sighs' as it was built in 1819 to enable the prisoners to be brought from the Galway Courthouse to the County gaol, which was then on the site of the present Galway cathedral. Then it was known as the Gaol Bridge.

# The Salmon Weir

One of the main features of Galway City is the preponderance of its waterways. To the visitor it must seem is if the whole place is afloat, but apart from the main river, the Corrib, most of these were commercial waterways, driving various mills and foundries. Not the least of these is or was the Eglinton Canal.

Opened in August 1852 by Lord Eglinton, or the Earl of Eglinton to give him his full title, the canal to which he gave his name took four and a half years to build. It was conceived as an idea to open up the rest of Conamara and South Mayo to trade with Galway and the outside world.

Previously the main trade route for any goods in this part of the country was to haul them overland as far as the coast and sail them down into Galway harbour, a roundabout and sometimes dangerous route in winter. True, materials could be brought down the river Corrib by steamer, but to get them to the sea for shipping on meant that they had to be unloaded at Woodquay, loaded onto horse carts and transported over land trough the city to the harbour.

Previously many attempts had been considered for such a canal and various routes were contemplated, including the actual digging of part of a channel between the Corrib and Lough Atalia around 1498 under the patronage of the mayor at the time, Andrew Lynch. That venture failed and became known thereafter as Lynch's folly.

Following the opening of the Eglinton canal, it enjoyed only a modest success as it was superseded by the Galway Clifden railway not long after its opening. There were five opening, or swing, bridges along the route and two locks, one at Parkavera and another at the Claddagh quay side of the basin to regulate the level of the water.

All of the swing bridges were finally replaced by permanent concrete bridges by 1954, and the canal ceased to exist as navigable water. It still provides a pleasant aspect and the roadway, which adjoins it, is a popular walkway.

There have been mutterings about reopening it by dreamers, but the sheer volume of road traffic today in the city would certainly prohibit the delays likely to be caused by the opening of swing bridges to allow the occasional craft to pass.

# Waterways of Galway

This thatched bar is situated in Eyre Street near the junction with Suckeen or Sickeen, now grandly called St Brendan's Avenue, and is better known to locals as 'The Hole in the Wall', a name it received from the fact that there was a hole in the wall of the back garden, which could be accessed from the yard of the old Garda Barracks in Eglinton Street. This, it is alleged, allowed the aforementioned guardians of the peace the opportunity to quietly slip through and indulge in the occasional libation without the publicity and the fear that their appearance might have given if they were seen to enter through the front door. Of course since those days the Garda barracks has moved to Mill Street and extensive rebuilding has long since demolished the wall, so the term 'Hole in the Wall' exists only in the memories of those old enough to remember. The building itself has been in the Fahy family for only about twenty years, before that it was known as Dick Fitz's after the then proprietor Richard Fitzgerald. The building itself is one of only two surviving thatched licensed premises in the city, the other being Cooke's Thatch Bar in Newcastle Road.

Neither of them could have been built within the City's walls as an ordnance at the end of the 16th century forbade the construction of houses of timber or thatch following a great fire which almost destroyed the town. It was following this that many of the fine stone buildings still to be seen throughout the city were built, and this is evidenced by the dates on many of the so called marriage stones, which date, in the main, from the end of the 16th century and the first fifty years of the 17th century.

Fahy's Pub

Galway is unique in having perhaps the largest colony of mute swans in the country. These beautiful birds sail in a majestic convoy every morning out to the shallows at the edge of the sea from the docks to the Renmore area. There they feed on the plentiful supply of weed, which they reach by tipping over and floating with their tails in the air, while with extended necks they pick away at the bottom with their orange beaks. When they have eaten enough, they cruise back on the rising tide in a long, graceful line arriving back in the Claddagh on the high tide. In recent times many people have taken to feeding the swans every day and now many of them don't put to sea at all, but hang about, looking beautiful, waiting for their benefactors, much to the delight of artists and photographers.

## LONG WALK

Originally known as the long wall, this was built around the end of the 16th century from the old docks, which were situated in the present fish market square in front of the Spanish Arch. Extending from the town wall to Crow Rock, this wall was undoubtedly built as a 'warping wall' to enable ships crews to pull their ships from bollard to bollard (a technique known as warping) against the strong river current to arrive at the old dock. Even today it is very difficult to sail a modern sailing boat up against this current, but in square-rigged ships, off the wind, it must have been virtually impossible. The evidence for the warping is the extreme wear on the upstream side of all of the remaining stone bollards. By

the middle of the 18th century a new dock was constructed, under the auspices of Edward Eyre, at the end of the wall (now known as the mud dock) and the wall was expanded and became known as Eyre's Long walk. Eventually through silting and by filling the ground at the back (East) of the wall, enough ground was created to build houses and the now familiar Long Walk, much beloved of painters, took shape.

Originally an unfashionable residential area Long Walk nowadays, with its many new apartments, is a very sought after address.

# The Swans at Long Walk

The famous fishing village across the river from Galway City, Claddagh (*An Cladach* – shore or stony beach) has been a town or village since the early Christian times, far older than Galway City itself. Originally a cluster of some 500 thatched cottages, scattered seemingly randomly, with crooked, winding roads leading down to the waterside. A thriving industrious fishing community, the Claddagh fisher folk supplied fish to the people of Galway and were granted a special status as a result. While the men caught the fish it was the women who sold it. Right up until the late 1950s it was common to see these shawl clad ladies carrying baskets of fish balanced on their heads, bellowing out their cries of 'Fresh macklers (Mackerel)', or 'Fresh herrins' in voices that could easily be heard a couple of streets away.

At the end of the 1920's a medical commission deemed Claddagh to be an unsanitary place, with its complete lack of running waters or sewers. As a result, the authorities compulsorily acquired the houses, and by 1934 they were demolished and replaced by the present neat rows of corporation houses. The Claddagh fishermen fished Galway Bay out of sailing boats known as Hookers because of the practice of using long line fishing techniques using miles of line and baited hooks. Highly superstitious, these fishermen would refuse to put to sea if in the morning if they saw a fox or a red headed women, and so any Claddagh girl afflicted with red hair, and there

were many, were forced to stay indoors until the fleet had put to sea.

Eventually most of the Claddagh boats were put out of business by the arrival of commercial trawling and steam and motor-powered boats. Today only a couple of dozen of the Claddagh men make any living from fishing.

A very close knit community, the Claddagh folk always ran their own affairs, separate from the laws and regulations of the Galway City fathers, electing their own 'King' who ruled like a high chief and had the last word in settling disputes etc.

Today a 'fashionable' area in which to live, many non Claddagh people are buying houses here and enjoying its wonderful sea and riverside location within minutes of the city.

# The Claddagh

This is the traditional fishing/ cargo sailing boat of the west coast of Ireland. The origin of its design though appears lost in time. There are many theories as to where the design originated; ranging from the Viking Longboat, Spanish Galleon, Dutch Hoeker, to the cutters and yawls of the south of England. None of these theories can be substantiated however and there is evidence that the design has at least been in existence here in Galway for several hundred years. A crude carving on a 18th century stone at Drumacoo Church bears an almost perfect resemblance to the present day boats except for the stern.

There is plenty of evidence of their existence since the beginning of the 19th century. Indeed there are a few hookers still sailing that are aged in the region of one hundred years, albeit altered and repaired over the intervening years.

The main distinguishing features are a high almost perpendicular prow, with a sharp clean entry curving gracefully to a full almost round belly with a distinctive curving tumble home (rounded flank) outboard of the gunwale line. The rig is known as a gaff rig and the large sails are still generally of a brown nature.

The boats come in four different types and sizes they are *Bád Mór* (Big Boat) approximately 40ft; *Leath bhád* (Half Boat) around 32 ft; *Gleóiteog* (pronounced Glowtyoge) about 25 ft; and *Púcán* (pronounced Pookaun) about the same length though rigged differently.

Between them these magnificent sailing craft were the lifeblood of the Claddagh fishermen and the Conamara fisher/turf traders. According to Richard J. Scott in his excellent book *The Galway Hooker* (Ward River Press 1983) a census taken in 1835 showed that a fleet of over 596 of these craft operated along the coast of Galway, giving work and sustenance to thousands of people during those hard years.

Nowadays only a fraction of these craft exist and most are engaged in sport sailing and cruising. Some thirty or so boats regularly compete in regattas from Conamara to Kinvara during the summer months, and rather than fading away, new boats are actually being built today giving rise to a revival of the craft of the traditional boat builder. Several of the smaller Gleóiteogs are to be seen regularly in the Claddagh area of Galway

# Galway Hookers

Mutton Island, which comprises some three acres of land, is just offshore from the mouth of the present harbour. The name probably derives from its use as common grazing land by the freemen of Galway as far back as 1664. At that time there was a castle or fortress on the island to protect the approach to the city from marauders from the sea. This was surrendered up to Sir Charles Coote, Cromwell's right-hand man, in April 1652 following the capitulation of Galway City.

Later again it was decided to rebuild this castle and construct a fort around it in 1691 with fourteen cannon on its walls. 1701 saw the completion of this work and the fort was garrisoned by troops recruited in Galway City for the purpose of fortifying the approaches to the bay.

With the increase of coastal and international trading by sea by the beginning of the 19th century, it was decided to build a lighthouse, together with a residence for the lighthouse keeper, on the site of the original castle/fort. This lighthouse remains until today and, although now operated automatically, the original residence still exists. It was inhabited up until the 1960s. In 1943 a local young man from the docks area, who was the sweetheart of the lighthouse keeper's daughter, was tragically drowned while attempting to deliver a message by rowing boat, which was swamped in bad weather.

Recently the subject of much legal wrangling and controversy, the island has now been connected for the first time to the mainland by a causeway and the new sewage treatment system for Galway City and surrounds has been erected there. It is hoped that its construction will assist in no small way in cleaning up the waters of Galway Bay.

# Lighthouse, Mutton Island

Although it now appears to be a part of Galway City, the seaside resort of Salthill is a comparatively new phenomenon. It began its life as a seaside resort in the middle of Victoria's reign and people began to go there in the summer to bathe, a new sport, and to indulge in the medicinal benefits of the seaweed baths which were operated by the Cremin family. They stood on the site of Seapoint and operated into the end of the 1940s. When Salthill was linked by horse drawn tram with the city centre in 1879 it became even more popular, and ordinary citizens could climb aboard a tram in Eyre Square and be transported out of the city within around a half an hour.

Originally it had the appearance of a separate village or town but gradually, as the population became more affluent, people began to build their houses out there and soon it had sprawled its way into Galway City. In the summer it was the place to go, with dancing, amusements and even Casinos of sorts. It was where we, as young boys, went to meet girls and they to meet us. Initially, the main dance hall was The Pavilion Ballroom, which had begun its life as a Royal Flying Corps aircraft hangar in the military airfield at Oranmore and was sold after the British army moved on in 1922. Of course the local populace never called it by its fancy new name and it was known to one and all as 'The Hangar'. Next came Seapoint Ballroom, a state of the art modern ballroom with a restaurant on the ground floor, which opened its door in 1950 and continues today as a leisure centre.

The Galway Lawn Tennis Club was, and still is, one of the main sporting venues, as is the Galway Golf Club which boasts a wonderful 18 hole links course in Pollnarooma. The seaside resort is still as popular as ever, with Leisureland entertainment centre and the Pearse Stadium contributing to sport and relaxation. A favourite pastime of all Galwegians is to walk the prom as far as Blackrock and kick the wall before returning.

Salthill

Sometimes spelt Spiddle, this village and its people are very proud of its unofficial title of principal town of the Gaeltacht. Most of the population here speak Irish as their first language and actively do all they can to keep Irish as the spoken language of the village.

Situated about 10 miles west of Galway the village gets its name from the Irish word *Ospideal*, or hospital, and it is thought that there was a hospital for lepers here probably on the site of the ruins still visible in the grounds of St. Eanna's Church. The Church itself is a fine example of the Celtic Romanesque style which was popular with architects during the Celtic renaissance at the turn of the 19th and 20th centuries. It was designed by William A. Scott, and contains some fine windows by Sarah Purser.

Spiddal was the family seat of the Morris family, the Lords Killanin, the 3rd of whom, Michael, was the Chairman of the International Olympic Games Committee. He sold the fine granite Spiddal House in 1960 to an American. Another famous son of the village was the boxer Máirtín Thorton who had the status of a folk hero in the 1940s.

As well as the Irish language Spiddal has, for many years, been one of the heartlands of traditional Irish music and has produced many, many fine musicians and singers. Perhaps one of the best slow air tin whistle players ever was the late Festy Conlon who died in 2001. His mother, Mamó as she was known, was an inspirational folk singer. Throughout the 1950s, 1960s and 1970s it was the Standún family that kept the music alive and still today one of this family, Dearbhal, is one of the world famous group Altann and a formidable fiddle player in her own right.

The beach, pier and blue blue waters make this a favourite tourist place in summer and it also plays host to hundreds of young Irish adults learning Irish in the summer months. The craft centre known as *An Ceardlann* is well worth a visit for the excellence and variety of the craftware to be seen and bought there.

# Spiddal Coast

This is perhaps one of the finest tower houses in the entire county if not the country. Dating from around 1500, it was the stronghold of the native Irish family the O Flaherty's who owned and controlled much of the land outside the walls of Galway to the West. Indeed it is often said (though not yet proven) that on the West gate of Galway city there was a prayer cut in stone which read *'From the ferocious O Flaherties, Good Lord deliver us'*. The castle, which has two bawns or enclosures, is six floors high with two bartizans on the corners of the 3rd floor. It has now got a new beautifully restored roof which was done in recent times by the O.P.W. using as a model Dunsaughlin castle near Dublin, which is the only castle in the country to retain its original roof.

Northeast of the castle there is a dock within the bawn, from which the O Flahertys would sail onto Lough Corrib.

To the south of the main castle are the remains of the banqueting hall, which nowadays only comprises the east wall and part of the north and south walls. There are some very fine carvings of a grain and grape motif over the semi circular window reveals of this wall.

It is said that there was a tilting stone in the floor of the banqueting hall over which the O Flahertys would place the seat of their guest at the banquet. If he was somebody that they liked all was well but if, however, he happened to be somebody they wished to dispose of a secret bolt was pulled and the hapless victim was despatched into the river which ran through a cave below the floor.

The floor, and with it the rest of the banquet hall eventually collapsed into the river, and we shall never know if the story is true until it is someday excavated. Aughnanure Castle is now in the capable hands of Duchas, the Heritage Service, and is open to the public in the tourist season.

# Aughnanure Castle

# The People of Galway

Surprise in any age can be divine. Thus, when the first people came upon the estuary of the River Corrib in the heart of County Galway all these years ago, amazement filled their eyes.

These Mesolithic or Middle Stone Age food gatherers were tired when they made their find; long days had been spent wandering the shorelines with only meagre food returns - suddenly, in the shallow estuarine waters before them, bass, mullet and salmon flashed a welcome not easily ignored. Shell and flat fish were in abundance also and in the deeper river channel waters, masses of eels converged. Culinary desires were quickly sated as these nomads became the first inhabitants of these Corrib lands over seven thousand years ago. We are here since!

In time, their wide variety of spear and arrow heads, scrapers and even knifes, made of dark chert stone from nearby Menlo, have been found on the now submerged shorelines of that ancient era. Time, as ever, passed on and by 4000 B.C. new stone technologies arrive on the Galway scene - large axeheads of chert on the same river shorelines tell of newcomers intent on harvesting the land. These Neolithic or New Stone Age settlers, our first farmers, cleared the forests on either side of the River Corrib with their primitive tools and have left an even greater legacy in the crumbled outline of a megalithic (large stone) tomb of the portal dolmen type in the nearby townland of Angliham. Still to be excavated, this 5000 year old house of the dead is Galway City's oldest building!

With the arrival of the Bronze Age to these western territories, about 2000 B.C., implements of bronze and copper made their appearance, suggesting a new influx of farmers who also sought metal deposits in areas around Cong on the northern end of Lough Corrib. However, as the Bronze Age drew to a close about 400 B.C., newcomers again appeared in these Corrib territories. This time they left an indelible mark on the landscape as well as on the generations to come.

These Iron Age people swept across the country

# Galway People

and brought a Celtic culture with them which found sustained nourishment amid the rocky low-lands of Connemara west of the Corrib and on the Aran Islands. Today, the Gaelic language flourishes in these areas which we call the Galway Gaeltact, or Irish speaking district, the largest in the land. Some local electoral areas in Galway City find themselves in this category also and organisations like *Gaillimh le Gaeilge* (Galway with Irish) promote the spread of this important aspect of our ancient culture in a city founded, ironically, by French-speaking foreigners much later, in the 13th century.

The Celtic culture touched on many things, however, and fire, earth and water played a big part in their strange beliefs. The Druids were the priests or engines of these rituals in which worship of the seasons, mother earth, sun, trees and streams were central themes of their devotion. Surprisingly, and after the passage of so much time, subliminal manifestations of Celtic beliefs still linger in the Galway soul. Thus, on May Day each year, May bush branches appear over outer doors in the older inner city areas, reflecting ancient devotion to Bealtaine the first great Druidic feast of the year. Similarly, religious sites, now adopted by Christians, at water sources, such as St. Augustine's Well at Lough Atalia beside the city's docklands reflect back to Celtic times when water was looked on as the key to life itself.

Yet, there was also a darker side to the Celtic character, manifested by the La Tène type iron sword recently retrieved from the River Corrib. These Celts were a warlike people also, as the profusion across the Galway landscape of their farmsteads surrounded by circular mounds of earth and ditches, known as Ringforts, readily testify. Although seven of these ancient monuments once lay inside the borough area of Galway City only those at Ballybane, the university campus at Dangan and adjacent to the Galway Racecourse at Ballybrit, remain. One, with the rather colourful name of *Rath Ún*, (The Fort of Ún), now vanished under a housing estate, gave the title Rahoon to a suburb on the west bank of the River Corrib.

The most spectacular of the Celtic forts were those huge stone constructions found in each of the three Aran Islands. *Dún Aengus* (The Fort of Aengus) on Inishmore, the largest of the islands, is the most prominent. This massive semi-circular monument on the very edge of the sheer Atlantic cliffs, with high stony ramparts and strengthened by outside walling complete with a chevaux-de-frise set of enclosing stones, dates from the time of Christ and is just one of many such monuments on these islands at the entrance to Galway Bay.

Not surprisingly, the arrival of Christianity in the 5th century impinged on these Celtic kingdoms set up by builders of the major forts. The Aran Islands became known as 'Aran of the Saints' when young men came to study and join the monastic way of life. St. Enda was the pioneer of this surge of monastic endeavour on the islands and the subsequent ruined oratories we see today remind us of the longevity of piety on these bare rocks where the founders of Clonmacnoise and even Iona itself first studied the Word of God.

Elsewhere, many of these early Christian monastic sites grew in size and stature, a number being founded on either side of Lough Corrib as well as on its islands. In this regard, for instance, tradition tells how the nephew of St. Patrick himself came to Inchagoill, *Inis an Ghaill Criabhthigh* (The Island of the Devout Stranger), today the most visited island in the upper lake. Here, we are told, he founded his monastery which today boasts two ancient churches, St. Patrick's Church with its trabeate doorway and the later Church of the Saints with its delightful Hiberno-Romanesque equivalent. Nearby stands the famous Luguaedon Pillar-stone, inscribed with twenty-three Old Latin characters which read,
LIE LUGUAEDON MACCI MENUEH,
(The Stone of Luguaedon, the Son of Menueh). Standing about a metre high, this stone contains some of the earliest writing in the land and is described as one of the more interesting pillar-stones in the Irish context.

The most famous of the native Corrib monks was St. Furse, who was born in 584 on nearby Inchiquin, an island now joined by a causeway to the major angling marina at Greenfields. On the road back to Headford are Killursa church ruins and cemetery, which bear his name, but it is at Peronne in France that this great Irish saint has left his mark as well as on the famous visions of Dante, many centuries later.

Further south, another Irish saint sought solace on these Corrib lands, for at lovely Annaghdown on the eastern shores of Lough Corrib lies another ecclesiastical site of major importance. Tradition is working overtime yet again for here in the 6th century, we are told, no less a person than St. Brendan, the Navigator, came to build a convent for his sister and find some peaceful rest from his many travels. Sadly, he also died there in 577 and, not surprising, a large monastic site including a priory granted to the Arroasian nuns and a later cathedral were founded in these lovely settings. Today it is worth the short journey from Galway City alone to view the magnificent Hiberno-Romanesque window in the ruined cathedral, which led Richard Hayward to pen these words about those exciting times in Galway's history:

*"......, when Irish craftsmen evolved a really native style of architecture and left as a memorial of their genius such fertility of conception, and such variety*

# Galway People

Today, nothing suggests an early Christian past in the centre of Galway City, but take a short trip to its eastern suburbs of Roscam and be prepared for quite a shock. Here, on the shores of Galway Bay lies a huge monastic enclosure, its extent only appreciated when viewed from the air. Rising from its centre is an unfinished Round Tower of perhaps the 10th or 11th century, and nearby lie the remains of a later church. Not surprisingly, the sense of devastation lies all around, when Galway's first recorded visitors, the Vikings (Norsemen), crashed ashore here in 807. They attacked all such sites along the shorelines of Galway Bay, reaching as far south and inland as Kilmacduagh with its famous leaning Round Tower, as early as 866.

Conscious of the wealth of so much monastic sites in the lands of the Corrib, one wonders what took them so long to come and wreck their particular brand of pagan havoc on monastery and monk alike. The year 927, however, records these fierce raiders ravaging the holy places about Lough Corrib. Again one wonders why they did not establish one of their permanent settlements (like Dublin) on the Corrib estuary, an ideal base for further plunder. Perhaps the natives here were just too unfriendly!

Things were changing for these Vikings invaders, however, because with the advent of a new millennium, we find these Norsemen settling down in Ireland and, after the Battle of Clontarf in 1014 and their defeat by the High King, Brian Boru, they seep quietly into the Irish way of life. These new times also saw changes in the administration of the church with the demise of the old monastic ways in favour of the diocesan system. As the second millennium gathered pace, new Religious Orders began to arrive led by the Cistercians who founded the first abbey on Galway soil at Abbeyknockmoy in 1189-90 under the patronage of Cathal Crovdearg O'Connor, King of Connacht. Abbeys and priories also began to appear about the Corrib country, with the Augustinians arriving at Cong and Annaghdown shortly afterwards and the Franciscans at Claregalway about 1250 and at Ross Errilly near Headford a century later. Said to be the most extensive (it has two cloisters) and best preserved of the Franciscan friaries, Ross Errilly today towers above a sheep-filled Corrib landscape, its memories locked for ever in the deep waters of the nearby Black River. It is a sad example, however, of the ruination that followed the suppression of the monasteries and religious wars of the 16th and 17th centuries. Yet, these ruins recall a time of prosperity, when monks prayed in peace and worked the land around them, employing the latest in farming techniques.

Their decline can be traced back to events which occurred much earlier, when Norman invaders under Strongbow landed in Ireland in 1169 and gradually spread their might across a troubled country. It began for Galway in the year 1235, when Richard de Burgo gathered his forces around him on the brow of what is now Prospect Hill above Eyre Square. Finding little opposition from the O'Flahertys, the local chieftains, who were banished across the Corrib, these Norman invaders set about founding a settlement on the east bank of the estuary. With sea, river and swamp providing protection on three sides, they quickly erected a wall on the open east end, thus securing the chosen site from any dissident Irish attack. Consequently, while the other eleven Norman towns envisaged for County Galway never really prospered, Galway did because of its powerful defence structures. Today, portions of this first curtain wall can be seen in the Eyre Square Shopping Centre, and is a stony testament to these testing times, which saw the medieval town of Galway take root behind these stout defensive features.

In time a local, as well as international, market economy grew up within these walls, with farm produce such as wool, leather and fish being exported through its initial port near the Spanish Arch. In return, wines, brandies, spices, iron and a whole range of goods were imported through these medieval quays and piers which still lie almost intact beneath the open plaza we see there today. Trade, then, became the throbbing heart of this new settlement on the very edge of the western world and in time fourteen merchant families, consisting of the Athys, Blakes, Bodkins, Brownes, Darcys, Deanes, Fonts, Frenchs, Joyces, Kirwans, Lynchs, Martins, Morrises and Skerretts became the prominent rulers of the medieval port, which became, for a period, the third most important in these isles after London and Bristol!

Later known as the Tribes of Galway, a derogatory term used by a rather indignant Cromwellian officer, those fourteen families were not, as one would imagine, of native stock, but formed the bulk of the Norman colony set up by de Burgo might. They gradually formed themselves into an exclusive aristocratic ruling class, adopted coats of arms without heraldic authority and contrived, by various edicts, to keep the town exclusively English so that *"neither O ne Mac should strutte ne swagger through the streets of Galway"*. Of these famous Tribal families, the Lynch family was the most powerful in wealth, culture, influence and civic spirit but, if the truth was told, most of these merchant families became some of the richest in the land. In time, when Galway reached its zenith as a city state, always loyal to the Crown but running its own affairs, it became so rich and famous that *"as proud as a Galway merchant"*

# Galway People

became a proverb which entered freely into continental gossip.

Pride then was a necessary ingredient of these Galway merchants and, not surprisingly, the Tribes acquired nicknames with, appropriately, the proud Lynchs taking pride of place. The Lynchs had every reason to be proud, of course, because as well as providing eighty-four mayors to the city, they built many of the fine stone mansions whose fragments dot the inner city area today. International trade was the basis of their success and family members became established as wine producers in places like Bordeaux, where an emigre Lynch founded the Lynch-Bajes vineyard, while later Lynchs possessed vast estates in Virginia and Maryland in the New World. An American Lynch went on to sign the American Declaration of Independence, but the best known Lynch/American connection is sadly based on fiction in the shape of the Lynch Memorial Window monument in Market Street. From this two (originally three) light window, legend tells how Mayor James Lynch hanged (lynched, according to American telling!) his own son over a *crime passionelle* at the end of the 15th century. However, and rather surreptitiously, the window was modified in the 19th century to fit in with this dark legend, and provides today the world's first official tourist trap!

The remaining Tribal families also have stories to tell, such as the merry Joyces, who gave their name to Joyce Country in Connemara after the first of their clan, a Welshman, settled there in the 13th century. Henry Joyce was mayor of Galway in 1542, while the Rev. Henry Joyce had the famous 1651 Pictorial Map of Galway engraved. Today, the Joyce connection is commemorated in their famous mansion, Tara Hall in Mervue, now the seat of Royal Tara China Ltd. Meanwhile, the brave Brownes supplied many members to the mayoral office, owned extensive properties, especially in County Mayo, and are remembered mostly from the famous Browne Doorway, which graces Eyre Square, after being removed from Abbeygate Street in 1905.

The litigious Martins, first noted as major millers in medieval Galway, had many members who also wore the mayoral chain, as well as famous characters such as Nimble Dick who, despite fighting against William of Orange, was still granted practically all the O'Flaherty lands in Connemara (thus the 'nimble' adage!); Richard Martin, known as Humanity Dick who founded the Society for the Prevention of Cruelty to Animals and Edward Martyn of Tullira Castle who, among other things, helped found Sinn Féin, the Abbey Theatre, the Palestrina Choir and Tullira Castle as it is known today.

The prating Frenches who also supplied a number of mayors to Galway, acquired much property throughout Connacht and a memorial slab to Sir Peter French and his wife, Maria Browne, can be seen in the Franciscan graveyard in Newtownsmyth in the heart of the city. The Blakes, on the other hand, leave more substantial monuments in Galway City, among which are Blakes Castle opposite the Spanish Arch, and Menlo Castle, soon to be restored. Owners of vast estates throughout County Galway, this family saw Sir Richard Blake become chairman of the Confederation of Kilkenny in 1647.

Not so becoming are the bloody Bodkins, who obtained their unhappy description from a family tragedy in the 18th century. While the Fonts and the Deanes left little impact on either the history (Edmond Deane in 1503 was the family's only mayor) or the archaeology of the city, the Athys at least left their famous doorway dating to 1577, now in the city museum.

The Kirwans, on the other hand, who have given their name to a famous lane in Galway's city centre and whose 'Chateau Kirwan' wine still flows freely in Bordeaux, were major merchants who lost much property in the Cromwellian confiscations. Some conformed and prospered as did Richard Kirwan of Cregg who became a renowned chemist at the end of the 18th century. The Skerrets also supplied many mayors to Galway and were prominent in ecclesiastical affairs, with two members becoming Archbishops of Tuam, while the Morris family, although not a predominant Tribe initially, were perhaps one of the best in overcoming the vicissitudes of Elizabethan, Cromwellian and Williamite Wars. Members of the family, although Catholic, reached high positions in the 19th century including parliament and one even became Lord Chief Justice for Ireland.

These then were the famous Tribes who started as merchants in medieval Galway. They were determined to succeed commercially, and to bring prosperity to their special settlement, which the natives had already begun to call *Gaillimh*, (The place of the Strangers). By 1484 this unique collection of Galway merchants had petitioned successfully to appoint the city's first mayor (Pyerse Lynch) by royal decree and even acquired the city's own ecclesiastical freedom from native Irish rule. They also acquired papal permission to appoint a warden to administrate their parish church dedicated to St. Nicholas, in the English fashion, behind what was then some of the finest city walling in the land. Naturally, both mayor and warden were appointed annually by these merchant princes, who married internally to keep control of both municipal and ecclesiastical election processes within that early golden circle!

European markets beckoned, of course, and with the visit in 1477 of Christopher Columbus to *"the Galway of Hibernia, where he saw sights, which told him that there was land beyond the seas"*, Galway's reputation as a seaport was made more secure. Today, a delightful stone sculpture commemorating this visit, a gift from Genoa, the great explorer's place of birth, is displayed by the Spanish Arch, – testimony, indeed, to the growing financial importance of this seaport in the exciting era of the sail.

The city's wealth had to be displayed, of course, and one of the main indulgences of its merchant princes was the manner in which they embellished their homes with carved stone, internally on fireplaces, and externally on the front facades facing the streets. The stone used was the favourite local light blue limestone (now turned grey after centuries of weathering), while the masons were the most skilled craftsmen in their trade. This unique architectural development in stonework is best noted by Sir Oliver St. John who visited Galway in 1614:

*"The towne is small, but all is faire and statelie buildings, the fronts of the houses (towards the streets) are of hewed stone, uppe to the top, garnished with faire battlement, in a uniform course, as if the whole towne had been built upon one model. It is built upon a rock, environed almost with the sea, and the river; compassed with a strong walle and good defences after the ancient manner."*

According to the later 1651 Pictorial Map of Galway, some fourteen remarkable edifices, castles or mansion houses, of the nobility, gentry and citizens of Galway were also to be seen, and, with the Church of St. Nicholas, broke the uniform course of the town's skyline. Today, only Lynch's and to a lesser extent, Blake's Castles, as well as the Collegiate Church of St. Nicholas, survive.

Lynch's Castle in Shop Street, now an important branch of the Allied Irish Bank, has been described as the finest surviving town-castle in Ireland. Recently conserved by the bank, this remarkable edifice, with carved arms of the Lynchs, King Henry VII, and the Earls of Kildare, dates from the late 15th or early 16th century. Home, perhaps, to some of the many Lynch mayors of Galway, it later became a chandler's shop, before being acquired by the Munster and Leinster Bank (now a branch of the Allied Irish Bank) in the 1920s. Much of the rest of its facade is embellished with intricate stone carving, especially on the hood mouldings about its windows, while its gargoyles at roof level contain some fine carvings of heads closely paralleled on nearby St. Nicholas's Collegiate Church.

Blake's Castle, dating from the 15th or 16th

century, stands at the end of Quay Street, and once overlooked the city wall and nearby harbour. Today, only the front facade and portions of the side walls remain, incorporating windows, crenellations and machicolations typical of the period, some of which were recently restored as part of the adjacent Jury's Inn development. The castle was later used as the town jail, a store, and now houses a favourite Galway restaurant.

As well as these two monuments, St. Nicholas's Collegiate Church also survives to give us more than an inkling of the city's proud past. Dating from 1320, the original parish church has been much enlarged and embellished down through the centuries by the merchant princes of Galway. It goes without saying that the Lynchs led the way in this and added an extra nave and later an aisle under which many family members await their Redeemer. Memorials and memories of the past fill its hallowed space, including a memorial slab to a crusader, and the tradition of a visit from Christopher Columbus in 1577 (local lore, and, sadly, some publications, claim he made the visit during his famous voyage to America!). As a result of the religious conflicts of the 16th and 17th century, the building changed hands many times. Today the Church of Ireland enjoys service there, but in truth, its a rather special place for all who are proud of an ancient building that has served the city well in its long, and troubled history.

Trouble, of course, was never far away from a settlement of strangers set among the lands of a defeated foe. Internal conflict was present also, as we see in one of the first edicts issued by Pyerse Lynch, the first mayor. The de Burgos, now known as Burkes (Bourkes in County Mayo!), were banished to their Terryland Castle on the banks of the River Corrib outside the city walls. In time, the family fragmented into many sections, an important branch going to Portumna where they built a rather impressive seat, while the rest descended into revolt, becoming Irish in manner and demeanour with each passing year. It was the latter who erected many of the Tower Houses which claim attention on the Galway landscape. The O'Flahertys, too, began to occupy similar seats of resistance such as the impressive Aughnanure Castle, now a major tourist attraction, overlooking Lough Corrib near Oughterard.

External affairs began to impinge on the cultural, religious and economic life of Galway, starting with the Reformation and the Suppression of the Monasteries, which saw the fortunes of the Dominican, Augustinian and Franciscan churches directly outside the city walls go into decline, culminating in the eventual demolition of the former two and the latter being turned into a courthouse. Another factor which hindered the city's special trade with Spain was the Spanish Armada debacle of 1588.

# Galway
## People

This led to the local English garrison erecting a bastion beside the medieval dockland to guard against the city's main international trading partners! In time, an arch, ironically called the Spanish Arch, was opened at this point of the city wall leading down to new land being reclaimed from the estuary at Long Walk. Today, this arch is part of the city's municipal museum.

The 17th century, however, bestowed the greatest disasters on the proud city and its merchants with two civil wars devastating not only trade and property, but also the will to continue when civil as well as religious liberties of the majority of its citizens were set aside in the aftermath of defeat. The first of these, the Parliament versus Crown conflict, saw the royal city besieged for nearly nine months, before it eventually capitulated to Cromwellian troops under General Coote. The aftermath makes unpleasant reading as 17th century ethnic cleansing came into play. The expulsion of its citizenry, some deported in penal servitude to the West Indies, and the confiscations of property and violation of churches, including the Church of St. Nicholas, followed in a most shameful chapter of Galways history. The final humiliation came when many of the fine houses of the merchants were given as payment to Cromwellian personnel unused to such grandeur as a contemporary noted:

*"Soldiers that ought to content themselves with one cellar had great houses to live in till they burnt all the lofts and vaunscots and partitions thereof, and then remove to another house till they made an end of all the town".*

Some years later, in 1657, the Rev. R. Easthorpe wrote:

*"Poor Galway sitteth in the dust and no eye pitieth her. Her merchants were princes and great among the nations, but now the city which was full of people is solitary and very desolate."*

Galwegians, if anything, are tenacious and, when the attempted plantation of their city by good citizens from Gloucester *"whose integrity to the state would entitle them to be trusted in a place of such importance"*, failed, they bided their time to return. This came with the Restoration when many of the merchants regained their former properties and trade, if anything, began to blossom yet again. However, it was a false dawn. By 1691 as King William fought King James and as the Jacobite army retreated towards a sympathetic Galway after the Battles of the Boyne and Aughrim, frantic efforts were made to reinforce the city's defences. One can well imagine the urgency of the task in hand as the sound of Aughrim cannon rolled across the Galway countryside from the largest battle fought on Irish soil. Casualties of over 6,000 on that blood-soaked bog and hill soon brought home the reality of the situation to the beleaguered city, and after just a week of token resistance, the city gates were thrown open to Williamite forces to herald yet another downturn in Galway's topsy-turvy fortunes.

By now the die was cast and as draconian political, religious and economic measures were enforced against the majority of the population, most of the remaining merchants families bid adieu to their ancestral city and sailed away to Spain, Portugal, France, the West Indies and even American plantations already heavy with their presence from previous trading links. For those that remained in the city and surrounding areas, however, the incoming 18th century offered little consolation as the native Irish became mere tenants on Corrib lands they helped nurture from time immemorial.

The 18th century is best forgotten in our story because as other cities grew and expanded, their medieval hearts giving way to Georgian Squares and broad city centre streets, Galway stagnated. Commerce dwindled with the disappearance of the majority of the merchant class, which had made it such an important trade centre in earlier times. As a result, its street plans were never altered and that, as we shall see, makes Galway unique among the larger urban areas of Ireland today.

The advent of the 19th century brought new hope, however, as the Industrial Revolution saw prosperity settle on a new ruling class, this time industrialists, who brought jobs and industry to revive the fortunes of a city already fallen far behind lesser urban centres in both spatial and economic growth. Thanks to ample water power, the engine behind the Industrial Revolution, the city had over eighty water-based industries in seven industrial clusters operating throughout the 19th century. Huge distilleries, breweries, jute and paper factories, corn and wheat mills operated day and night, sending the population soaring to over 40,000, according to James Hardiman, the leading local historian of the day.

To house this huge influx of eager workers from outlying areas, the old medieval houses were modified, often lowered with new roofs added and always plastered as protection against the harsh western weather. New streets began to snake out from the medieval heart as worker and bosses alike sought accommodation. Municipal buildings such as hospitals, workhouse, courthouse and even a jail, were augmented by ecclesiastical endeavour as Dominicans, Augustinians, and Franciscans competed with the secular clergy in the race to provide churches when Catholic Emancipation in 1829 added greatly to the growing optimism. A new harbour at a cost of £40,000 augured well for international trade, while across the estuary, the old

# Galway People

fishing village of the Claddagh welcomed new boating facilities for its extensive fleet of Galway Hookers and other fishing vessels.

The blow when it came, arrived gently on the soft summer breeze of 1845 when the dreaded potato blight descended on greening stalks that stretched from the Aran Islands all the way to Annaghdown. The rest, of course, is history as the city and adjacent countryside saw thousands die of hunger during the Great Famine, which was to last over five long, dreadful years. The authorities did their best to cope but, with workhouse and fever hospitals filled with the afflicted, over 10,000 inhabitants perished in a decade. Thankfully, the provision of soup kitchens, as well as road, canal (Eglinton), river embankment, railway, university and Great Southern Hotel constructions helped to feed many families who otherwise would have perished. However, the damage, mentally as well as physically, was done. Galway's industries failed as demand for home produce petered out, while cheaper and often better made products came on the new railway line from Dublin to flood its dwindling market. Thus, the promise of economic redemption through industrial endeavour lay shattered in the dying embers of the 19th century. Only 14,000 citizens remained to meet the promise of the new one as unemployment and emigration took a terrible toll.

Even in the darkest times, however, a new dawn brings fresh hope, and as the 20th century spread across a chastened Galway and its hinterland, the embers of endeavour glowed again. New ideas of nationhood were now afloat in the aftermath of Land League successes, and as the nation looked to the glory of its Celtic past, Galway was in the vanguard of its revival. While politics ordained the need to fight for freedom, Galway was second only to Dublin in the risings of 1916, the city sought to paint a wider canvas of that unique past. The promotion of the Irish language through town and gown, through a vibrant Gaelic League and the promptings of a little man called Pádraic O'Conaire, whose limestone statue graces Eyre Square, saw the city do just that. Not far away, in Coole Park, the remnants of Old Decency cut a different furrow to the past with Lady Gregory not only recording Irish folklore for posterity, but also with W.B. Yeats from nearby Thoor Ballylee and Edward Martyn from Tullira Castle sowing the seeds of the Irish National Theatre in Doorus House on the nearby shores of windswept Galway Bay.

Meanwhile, the fight for independence in the early 1920s was often as bitter in the Galway region as elsewhere. The dogs of war spared neither side, but when peace finally arrived, it came at a price. The local economy was in tatters and many an Irish hope boarded ocean liners that seemed to fill Galway Bay up to the Second World War with depressing regularity. Ironically, a lack of passengers and freight forced the Galway/Clifden railway line to close in 1935. World War brought even further economic depression to the city, as its harbour ceased to operate and the commercial life ground mostly to a halt. Even at war's end and some years afterwards, economic life in Galway was at a low ebb, with very little industry present and much of the inner city areas such as Middle and Quay Streets, as well as Kirwan's and Buttermilk Lanes, little better than slums. Even today, life as in the latter, lives on in Walter Macken's poignant play, *Mungos Mansion*, an exposé of city life little different from that in other urban areas.

The start of the 1950s saw matters continue as before, but by the end of the decade a change for the better occurred. Perhaps, it was the winning of an All-Ireland Gaelic Football title in 1956 and the setting up of a welcome factory on land acquired by the Galway Chamber of Commerce and Galway Corporation in 1957 that saw the city's fortunes slowly change for the better. Since then, a whole plethora of industries, including service, have set up in four industrial estates, giving employment to over 10,000 workers today. Meanwhile, except for the main shopping spine through the heart of the city, the ancient centre area had become decidedly rundown. If things continued as they were, the inner

city, as a unit, would have withered slowly away and died within a decade. However, an enterprising government plan to encourage urban renewal was placed before Galway Corporation members towards the end of the 1980s.

The Tax Incentive Scheme for Designated Areas was a startling innovation and most welcome at the time. Simply put, various tax reliefs were made available for property renewal in chosen areas of the city. This meant that new developments, which brought commerce and people back to these rundown districts, had to maintain, if not enhance, the unique environment and heritage of the locality. By the end of the 1980s, before the first scheme was applied, the inner city area was a sorry sight. Outside of the main artery through its centre, many buildings lay in ruin, and those that were occupied or used as shops or small family businesses were covered in a rendering of 19th century plaster, often mossy green with dampness, and depressing to the eye. The once proud medieval heart had been besmirched by time itself. Sadder still, were the obvious gaps where proud merchants' homes once stood, echoes of Cromwellian ineptitude. Yet, the old medieval street plan lay intact as depicted in the 1651 Pictorial Map - all it needed was suitable urban development sympathetic with the past.

Today, the same street patterns exist, with nary a

street widened or straightened, as renewal gathered momentum in the 1990s, yet, always conscious of the past. That past became clearer with each passing year as the 19th century plaster rendering was removed to reveal the expert work of masons and builders of long ago. Looking back now, it easy to see how the Eyre Square Shopping Centre was the flagship of Galway's urban renewal schemes, when it started over a decade ago. Today, over fifty shops at two levels in the complex, a high-rise carpark capable of taking over 400 cars, and above all this, actual streets of houses (minus traffic!) seek reactions of the visitor to Galway's first venture into true urban renewal.

Then you see it. The old city wall, still standing there since c. 1270 when the Norman Conquest was in the balance, as O'Flahertys and O'Hallorans sought revenge for their expulsions. A long section of this ancient barrier stands high above the coffee shops and flea market in the Centre, augmented by two restored wall towers, named Shoemaker and Penrice, two of the original fourteen that once provided extra protection to the city's ancient fortifications. Built originally to keep strangers out, they now entice the visitor to come and shop!

Not that people need much enticing to come to Galway now that its urban renewal schemes have been mostly completed and its centre streets pedestrianised to capture yet again the gentle pace of the past. With many of the restored buildings containing restaurants and cafes offering international food to vie with the best, wine bars, night clubs and lively pubs have also come to flourish in a city that never really sleeps – except, it seems, mornings after the night before! Throw in its recently revamped riverside walks, the ambiance of nearby Lough Corrib and its connecting river, and you have a combination of Galway attractions irresistible to young and old alike.

Today, if you are an angling fan, Lough Corrib can be accessed from many points along its long and fretted shoreline. Countless little piers and modified inlets harbour hundreds of fishing boats allowing the angler to indulge in his favourite sport, while more conventional harbours can be found at Collinamuck, Birchall, Oughterard, Cornamona, Cong, Greenfields, Annaghdown and Galway City itself. For the general boating enthusiast, access can be gained from the places mentioned, but for the general visitor, lake excursion centres are usually confined to Galway, Oughterard and Cong. Yet, no matter how you go afloat on the Corrib, the exercise will not be in vain, as you ply the mysterious waters of the Republic's largest lake. While trout, salmon, pike, perch, roach and eel greet you from beneath the waves, the lake's stock of bird life will hold your attention also, especially when winter flocks of ducks and geese in particular fly in from places as far away as Canada, Iceland and Siberia.

History also greets you at every turn here on the western shores of the lake, as in the Parish of Killanin, which gave the title to the late Lord Killanin, head of the Morris family, another of the famous Tribes of Galway. Lord Killanin was President of the International Olympic Committee and presided over two Olympic Games. International affairs, however, are no stranger to these rolling wooded hills and smaller lakes which tease this western shoreline of the Corrib, for in this parish also lies Ross House, a delightful Georgian mansion built in 1777 by the Martins, another of the merchant families of Galway. Unlike so many of the other Tribes, this enterprising family was transplanted to the wilds of Connemara by the Cromwellian adventurers. In doing so, they finally displaced the long suffering O'Flahertys from their territories and, sadly, from history books forever. The international connection lies in the fact that Major Poppleton, described by Richard Hayward in his book, *The Corrib Country*, as one of the military gentlemen in charge of Napoleon when he was in exile on St. Helena, lies buried in the local graveyard. Married to one of the Martins, Poppleton brought back a gold snuff box, a gift from the famous prisoner, which later was found to contain letters for delivery to Napoleon's wife and son! Alas, at the time of their

discovery, Napoleon had already died. Here, also in this ancient house, lived Violet Florence Ross, who was co-author with Edith Somerville of important literary works in the fading twilight of the 19th century. One of these, *Some Experiences of an Irish R. M.* has since become the basis of the much-acclaimed 'The Irish R.M.' series, which lit up international television sets some years ago. In their 'The Big House of Inver,' they capture for ever life in the *Teach Mór* (Big House), this time Tyrone House overlooking Galway Bay, dormer home to the St. George family.

The film industry has also left its mark here with the 1970s film, *The Mackintosh Man*, featuring nearby Ardfry House.

Meanwhile, up on Corrib lands, as you leave Oughterard to head towards the Maam Valley and over to Cong on the northern end of this great lake, you enter 'The Quiet Man country'. Here, during a glorious six weeks' spell in 1951, Hollywood came to Galway in the shape of the famous film director, John Ford, who directed film stars John Wayne, Maureen O'Hara and Barry Fitzgerald in Ireland's best loved film called simply *The Quiet Man*. Amid this rolling Corrib countryside, The Duke (Wayne) fought the good fight over Maureen with the lovable, pugnacious Victor McLaghlan in scenes which still thrill thousands of Irish Americans, who come each year to walk the set. Naturally, Corrib Country has never been the same since!

Meanwhile, back down on the River Corrib, there are many delightful walkways, one leading up from the heart of the city to a rather mysterious folly in the shape of a stone teahouse, the last remaining memento of yet another Martin estate. Recently conserved by the Galway Civic Trust, it is now part of the local university's sports grounds. Across the river stand the ruins of Menlo Castle once a seat of the Blakes, another of the Tribes of Galway. The castle, in reality a castellated mansion incorporating an earlier 16th century tower house, was accidentally burnt in 1910 and today this most favourite of Galway ruins, awaits restoration amid the remnants of the once quite extensive Menlo Woods. In the words of poet W. P. Fogarty:–

*Around the ruined castle clings*
*The sad dim beauty of forgotten things*
*Roofless and open to the skies;*
*This treasured home deserted lies.*

Down in the inner city area a new riverside walk entitled *Bruach na Coiribe*, (Banks of the Corrib), has just been opened. It runs from Woodquay, which once contained the city's harbour, via a new walkway along the Middle River, all the way down to the old Mud Dock in the river's estuary, built by the Eyres,

Cromwellian supporters after whom Eyre Square is called, to replace the main medieval harbour upstream of the Spanish Arch. Along this route, one can enjoy the beauty of water in flow, as the River Corrib really gathers speed here, amid the reuniting of older waterways, which exit the main river further upstream.

Across the way stands the city's much discussed and, in the eyes of many, most impressive building, the 'Cathedral of Our Lady Assumed into Heaven and St. Nicholas', to give it its full title. This massive limestone building, whose design has been influenced by the classical tradition of Galway architecture of the period of the city's greatest prosperity in the 17th century and, in particular by its ancient Spanish affiliations, is laid out in the form of a cross; the nave of 300 ft. in length forms the vertical beam and the transepts represent the arms. The position of the altar is indicated by the dome directly over it, with the cupola rising to 145 ft. in height. A young building in the European context, the Cathedral's foundation stone was only laid in 1957 and the building was blessed and opened by Cardinal Cushing of Boston in 1965. Of interest is the fact that it was built on the site of the former county and city gaols. Its construction saw the last use of limestone on a massive scale in the Galway region, a stone which contrasts so well with the cathedral's unique combination of Connemara marble flooring and the rich glow of Canadian cedar wood in the roof.

Nearby, stands the original building of the National University of Ireland, Galway. This vast limestone quadrangle, (its design is loosely based on Christchurch College in Oxford), officially opened its doors to 68 students in 1849. Today, its campus encloses 250 acres stretching upstream along the River Corrib and caters for over 10,000 students, many of whom use the nearby waters for sporting and recreational purposes. Further downstream, the riverside walk finishes at the estuary where the Corrib River meets Galway Bay. Across what is locally known as The Quay Stream, the massive Nimmo's Pier (built in 1821 by Alexander Nimmo, a Scottish engineer) stretches out into the bay.

This is the start of yet another favourite walk out along what locals call 'The Prom'. This is a fascinating two-mile walk which provides many fine vistas of Galway Bay and the Burren Hills in the background. The first section lies along the edge of South Park, known locally as The Swamp – the sea regularly encroached here before Nimmo's Pier was built. It was here that women from the now demolished Claddagh fishing village once gathered bait. The park is now joined to Mutton Island by a recently constructed causeway while, on the island, beside one of Galway's most noted landmarks, its

lighthouse, is the city's new sewage treatment plant. Meanwhile, the walkway joins up with the Grattan Road Prom, originally built with the financial help of Lady Louise Grattan, in the 1860s as a massive causeway to retain the sea from flowing all the way in to Sea Road, where the Jesuit Church is today. Galway's largest beach, Grattan Beach, lies to the seaward side of the sea-wall. The end of this walkway joins up with the more recently constructed Seapoint Promenade, leading to the more famous Salthill Prom, which eventually finishes at the Blackrock Diving Tower after passing many more, smaller beaches on the way.

Salthill, Ireland's premier seaside resort, sports other delights such as Leisureland, an impressive recreational centre complete with public swimming pool, restaurant and a conference/ music/exhibition hall. Not far away, the once popular Seapoint Ballroom is now a leisure centre, beside Atlantamara, the resort's latest acquisition, a state-of-the-art sea aquarium specialising in native sea fish. Throw in a host of hotels, bars and clubs, with golfing and tennis facilities further out along The Strip and you see why Salthill is so popular today. Its not that too long ago that the resort was visited mostly by country people after the harvesting was done. They came simply for the chat and to avail of seabaths or even to drink the salty waters for that special cure. Times certainly have changed!

# Galway People

Enjoyment also comes further afield, for Galway Bay laps the sandy beaches and stony cliffs of the Aran Islands, a two-hour boat trip from Galway Docks or just over a half an hour from Rosaveal harbour, the same journey again by car from Galway out along the Coast Road (if traffic is light!). Alternatively, one could fly by Aer Arann from its own airport set along the rocky shoreline of Connemara and enjoy on the fifteen minute flight, an aerial view of these three stony jewels set amid a wash of blue. The three islands welcome thousands of visitors every year, each having its own attractions of massive Celtic forts, miles of stone walls and a Gaelic-speaking people time nearly forgot. Despite the summer flow of tourists, especially to Inismore, the largest of the three islands with its crowded pubs, restaurants and impressive heritage centre, there is still an old worldly ambience about the native Aran Islander, tuned to perfection by some of the older ladies on Inismean, the Middle Island, who still wear the red petticoat with native pride. There is a peace here as one tranverses tiny boreens lined by winding stone walls set amid rilled limestone sheets of simply huge proportions. A place time certainly forgot.

The same can be said of the Burren, that massive stony outcrop of County Clare, which verges the southern shores of Galway Bay. Here one can sense infinity, where once a Cromwellian officer lamented:

*There's not enough wood to hang a man,*
*Or water to drown a man,*
*Or earth to bury a man......*

Today Kinvara, directly across from Galway City and the last town in the county before you enter Clare, welcomes the tourist. Its Dunguaire Castle, a tower house was once owned by Richard Martyn, mayor of Galway in 1642, and is one of the major tourist attractions in the entire region. The great song composer, Francis A. Fahy, who wrote the old version of the song, 'Galway Bay' was born here and a unique gathering of the Galway Hooker sailing craft takes place every year. *Cruinniú na mBád* (the Gathering of the Boats) it's called, when the old sailing craft race again against themselves and the magic of the wave in Galway Bay, commemorating the old turf boats that once sailed here from Connemara with much needed fuel all those years ago. Here, at least, time does not forget!

Speaking of Connemara, its mountain wonders are only an hour's drive from Galway, but that's another story for another time. It's no wonder then that so many tourists flock to Galway City and its environs and why so many choose to retire there – it's that sort of place. Today theatre flourishes here, for Galway is the home of the Taibhdhearc, Ireland's theatre of the Gaelic language where such stalwarts of screen and play as Siobhán McKenna and Michael MacLimmor first trod the magic boards. Here you will find the four-times Tony Award winning Druid Theatre Company in its little lane off Quay Street, and not far way Macnas, the other internationally acclaimed theatre and street spectacle group, are already sounding drums for yet another Galway Arts Festival extravaganza.

Even here in a city, small by world standards, theatrical and musical groups face competition mostly unknown in cities of much larger sizes and populations. For Galway is also the City of Festivals - every month there seems to be a different one to suit the occasion. The famous Galway Races started the trend in the 19th century and poor Galwegians have suffered since. Regattas were next to tax the patience of employers, but now Oyster Festivals (two), Film Festivals, Arts Festivals, Music Festivals ..... the list grows endlessly in Galway, which, like Oliver, always asks for more!

Yet, there are peaceful spots in this city – you will them find amid the sad ruins of Menlo Castle, a short row up the Corrib. Meanwhile, down by the Claddagh, there is a strange serenity about swans floating in the backwaters of time itself, while not far away in Bowling Green, the ghosts of James Joyce and his beloved Nora haunt the little museum dedicated to them in the Barnacle home of not too long ago. Across the road, the tower of St. Nicholas's

Church casts a shadow on a very special window, whose ivy hides a murderous tale about the Lynchs, dark as legend itself.

Not far away, on even darker November nights, beneath the waters and the tide, thousands of lean black bodies turn slowly towards the open sea. These eels face a long, lonely journey back across the Atlantic to start the mystery of life all over again. Thousands of years ago, Stone Age people looked at their ancestors, and said simply, "Wow"!

# BIBLIOGRAPHY

Berry, Rev. J. Fleetwood B.D.: – *The story of St Nicholas' Collegiate Church, Galway.* (Facsimile edition, Church of Ireland Galway, 1989.)

Cearbhaill, Diarmuid, (ed.): – *Galway: Town & Gown 1484 – 1984,* Dublin, 1984.

Coen, Rev. Fr. Martin: – *The Wardenship of Galway,* Kenny's Bookshops and Art Galleries, Galway, 1984.

Fitzpatrick, Trish, and Whilde, Tony: – *Insider's Guide to Connemara,Galway and the Burren,* Dublin, 1992.

Gibbons, Erin, (ed.): – *Hidden Conamara,* Connemara, 1991.

Gosling, Paul: – *Archeological Inventory of County Galway,* Vol. 1, *West Galway:* Dublin, 1993.

Gwynn, A. and Hadcock R.N.:– *Medieval Religious houses Ireland,* Longman Group Ltd., London, 1970.

Harbison, Peter: – *Guide to National and Historic Monuments of Ireland,* Dublin, 1970.

Hardiman, James: – *The History of the Town and County of the Town of Galway (Dublin 1820),* Facsimile Edition, Kenny's Bookshops and Art Galleries, High Street Galway, Ireland, 1975.

Hayward, Richard: – *The Corrib Country,* Dundalk, 1943.

Joyce, Cecily: – *Claddagh Ring Story,* 1990.

Kavanagh, Mary: – *Galway - Gaillimh, A Bibliography of the City and County,* Galway, 2000.

Korff, Anne, and O'Connell, Jeff: – *Medieval Galway,* Kinvara, 1990.

Moran, Gerard, (ed.): – *Galway History and Society,* Dublin, 1996.

O'Dowd, Peadar, and Lawlor, Brendan: – *Galway - Heart of the West,* Galway, 1991.

O'Dowd, Peadar: – *Down by the Claddagh,* Galway, 1993; *Galway City,* Galway, 1998.

O' Dowd, Peadar : – *Old and new Galway,* Connacht Tribune and The Archeological, Historical and Folklore Society, Regional Technical College, Galway, 1985.

O'Flaherty, Roderic, (Hardiman, James, ed.): – *A Choreographical Description of West or H-Iar Connaught,* Dublin, 1846.

O'Neill, T. P.: – *The Tribes and other Galway Families,* Galway, 1984.

O'Sullivan, M. D.: – *Old Galway - The History of a Norman Colony in Ireland,* Cambridge, 1942, Galway 1983.

Robinson, Tim: – *Oileán Árann, a Map and Guide,* London, 1980.

Rynne, Etienne: – *Tourist Trail of Old Galway,* Galway, 1977.

Semple, Maurice: – *Some Galway Memories,* Galway,1973; *Reflections on Lough Corrib,* Galway, 1969.

Semple, Maurice: – *Where the River Corrib Flows,* Maurice Semple, 1988.

Spellissy, Seán: – *The History of Galway, City & County,* Limerick, 1999.

Walsh, Paul: – *Discover Galway,* Dublin, 2001.

Wilde, William: – *Loch Coirib,* Dublin, 1867.


Unpublished source material: – Richard J. Byrne, Craughwell, Co. Galway.

Dear Reader

This book is from our much complimented illustrated book series which includes:-

| | |
|---|---|
| Strangford Shores | Donegal Highlands |
| Dundalk & North Louth | Drogheda & the Boyne Valley |
| Armagh | The Mournes |
| Belfast | Fermanagh |
| Antrim, Town & Country | Omagh |
| Inishowen | South Donegal |
| Heart of Down | Limerick |
| East Belfast | Cookstown |
| Blanchardstown, Castleknock and the Park | Ring of Gullion |

For the more athletically minded our illustrated walking book series includes:-

Bernard Davey's Mourne          Tony McAuley's Glens
Bernard Davey's Mourne Part 2

Also available in our 'Illustrated History & Companion' Range are:-

City of Derry      Holywood      Ballymoney
Lisburn      Banbridge

And from our Music series:-

Colum Sands, Between the Earth and the Sky

We can also supply prints, individually signed by the artist, of the paintings featured in the above titles as well as many other areas of Ireland.

For details on these superb publications and to view samples of the paintings they contain, you can visit our web site at **www.cottage-publications.com** or alternatively you can contact us as follows:-

Telephone: +44 (028) 9188 8033      Fax: +44 (028) 9188 8063

*Cottage*
*Publications*

**Cottage Publications
an imprint of
Laurel Cottage Ltd
15 Ballyhay Road
Donaghadee, Co. Down
N. Ireland, BT21 0NG**